ALL I EVER NEEDED TO KNOW I LEARNED FROM

Jenn Fujikawa

Smart Pop Books

An Imprint of BenBella Books, Inc.

Dallas, TX

Smart Pop is an imprint of BenBella Books, Inc.
8080 N. Central Expressway
Suite 1700
Dallas, TX 75206
smartpopbooks.com | benbellabooks.com
Send feedback to feedback@benbellabooks.com

BenBella and *Smart Pop* are federally registered trademarks.

Printed in China
10 9 8 7 6 5 4 3 2 1

Library of Congress Control Number: 2024041778
ISBN 9781637743546 (print)
ISBN 9781637743553 (ebook)

Editing by Elizabeth Smith
Copyediting by James Fraleigh
Text design and composition by Aaron Edmiston
Cover design by Brigid Pearson
Printed by Dream Colour Printing Ltd.

MARVEL PUBLISHING
Jeff Youngquist, VP, Production and Special Projects
Sarah Singer, Editor, Special Projects
Jeremy West, Manager, Licensed Publishing
Sven Larsen, VP, Licensed Publishing
David Gabriel, VP, Print & Digital Publishing
C.B. Cebulski, Editor in Chief

**Special discounts for bulk sales are available.
Please contact bulkorders@benbellabooks.com.**

INTRODUCTION

Wise beyond its years, Marvel Comics has eighty-five years of storytelling under its belt. Throughout that time the characters have been through pretty much everything: saving the world and feeling accomplished one day; dealing with the worst of times, like suffering the immeasurable loss of a teammate, the next. From insurmountable challenges to victories beyond the realm of possibility, Marvel heroes have a multitude of relatable life lessons to teach.

Teamwork makes the dream work. Don't be afraid to fail. Being a hero is about more than strength. These lessons are classics for a reason and have an even deeper meaning through a Marvel lens. Take, for example, the Avengers, the ultimate team-up that shows even the hardest tasks can be completed with the help of others. Working together takes setting aside otherworldly egos for the good of the common goal (looking at you, Tony Stark).

In life, failure is always a possibility, but Peter Parker shows us the power of taking responsibility for one's actions. Through the loss of his beloved Uncle Ben, Peter learns to power through and grow up fast, making tough decisions on his own while still being a kid at heart. Sometimes it's impossible to know if you're making a wrong decision until you see the consequences, but you can look in the mirror and decide that you will handle the fallout like a true hero.

As for heroic actions in all forms, Jennifer Walters definitely knows what it takes to win a fight. As She-Hulk, her first reaction might be brute strength, but her courtroom experience has taught her that rational thinking and determination can often be the best way to win a battle. There are many avenues to solving conflicts, and being a hero is about using *all* of your skills—mental and physical—to find a solution.

From laughter and grieving to rebirth, and rebirth again and again—we all can't be Mr. Immortal, but we can learn a thing or two from the beloved and beleaguered heroes in Marvel Comics. Their actions are inspirational and their failures are cautionary tales. Through the eyes of our favorite characters, we can gain insight into our own lives to live heroically, no vibranium shield or Asgardian hammer necessary.

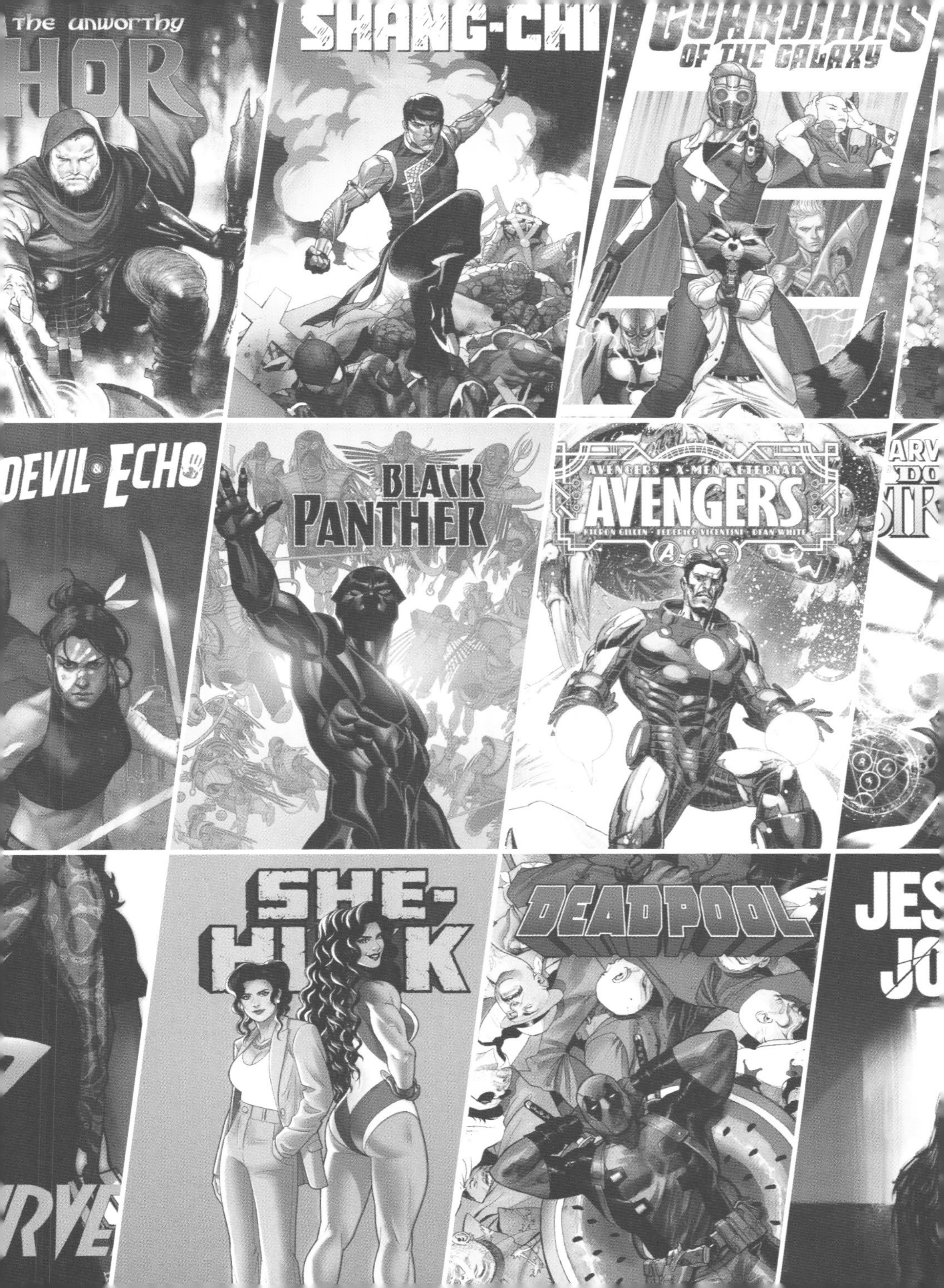

THE UNWORTHY
SHANG-CHI
OF THE GALAXY
DEVIL & ECHO
BLACK PANTHER
AVENGERS · X-MEN · ETERNALS
AVENGERS
KIERON GILLEN · FEDERICO VICENTINI · DEAN WHITE
DEADPOOL

WITH GREAT POWER THERE MUST ALSO COME GREAT RESPONSIBILITY

Even a web-slinger knows that difficult decisions come with a price. Teen genius Peter Parker's world transforms forever when he is bitten by a radioactive spider. With his enhanced abilities, he's able to climb walls and swing above the city, finally feeling free from the burdens of life. Except that he's not free: teenage life continues on. And Peter soon realizes that even for someone with super-powers, actions always have consequences.

When Peter first becomes Spider-Man, he revels in his powers. Then he sees a man committing a crime and lets him go because he feels it's not his job to take action. Getting involved isn't his problem. When that very thief later murders his Uncle Ben, only then does Peter understand the weight of his decisions—and of taking on the responsibility of being a true hero.

Super heroes or not, we make daily decisions that affect our lives and the lives of others. While it's impossible to know if you're making a wrong decision until you see the consequences, it's how you handle the fallout that is important. Great responsibility is a heavy weight to bear, but if you think beyond yourself, your own personal Spidey-Sense will help guide you to make the right choices.

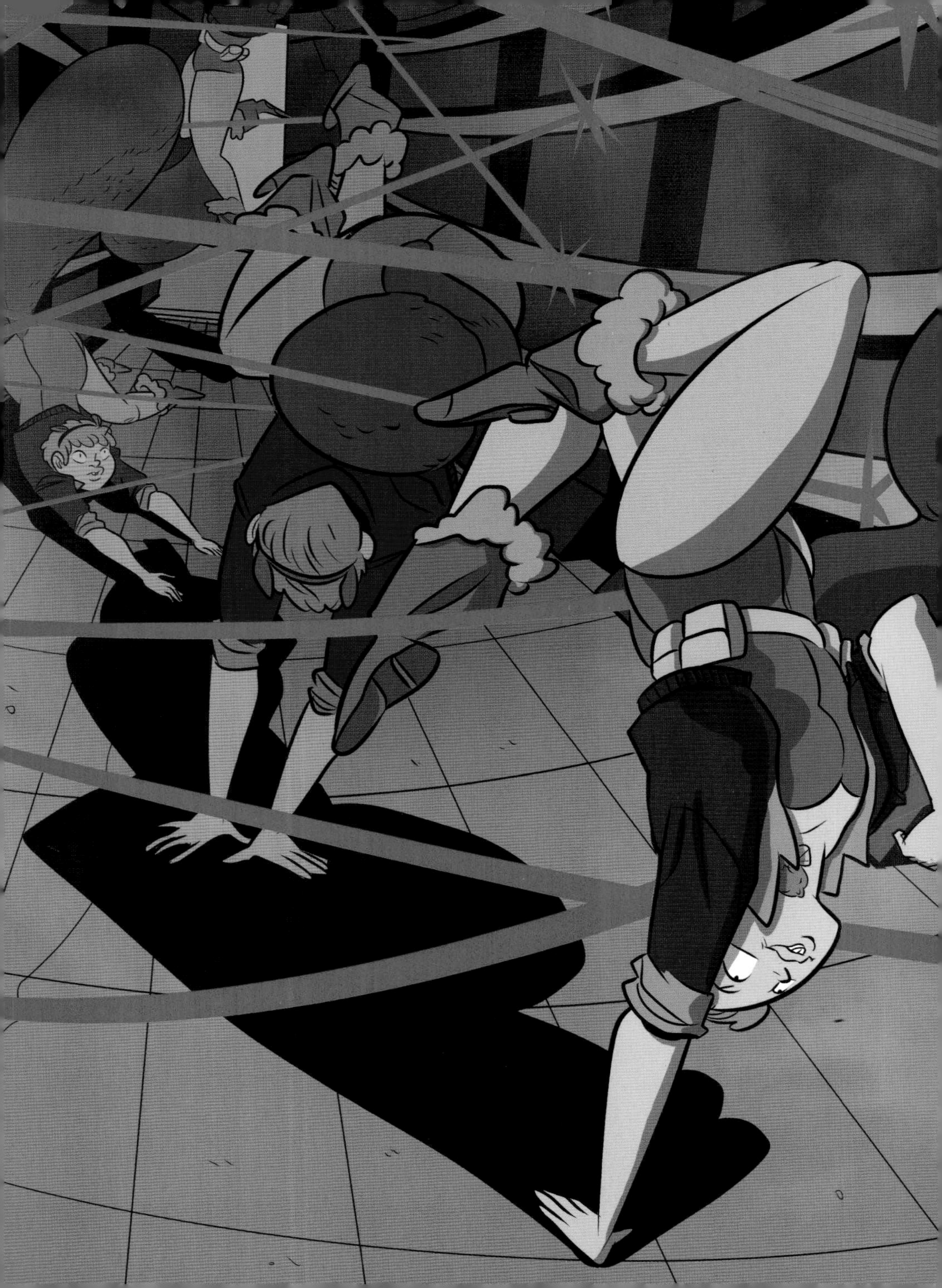

OPTIMISM CAN BE YOUR GREATEST STRENGTH

Self-confidence can make the impossible seem possible. As Squirrel Girl, Doreen Green is as nimble as her name, with enhanced strength and ability in hand-to-hand combat as well as a heightened sense of balance—not to mention her super-cool, unique ability to communicate with squirrels. As if those skills weren't impressive enough, she has a secret weapon: her irrepressible optimism.

Doreen's life turns upside down when Melissa Morbeck reveals Squirrel Girl's real identity. Not only do the villains she previously defeated form an alliance against her, she is also forced to face the world without the cover of her super hero persona. Yet somehow through it all, Doreen remains her positive, upbeat self—a gift that helps her learn to embrace her dual identity.

It's easy to underestimate someone who is naturally joyful and has a generally sunny outlook on life. This cheerfulness and enthusiasm can seem out of place in a world filled with pain and despair, whether it's a super hero story or the real world. But don't dismiss bright-eyed, bushy-tailed positivity; optimism should not be mistaken for naivete. So, channel your inner squirrel and go nuts! Take your unbeatable attitude and show the world what you've got. You'll be surprised at how it can pull you through any situation.

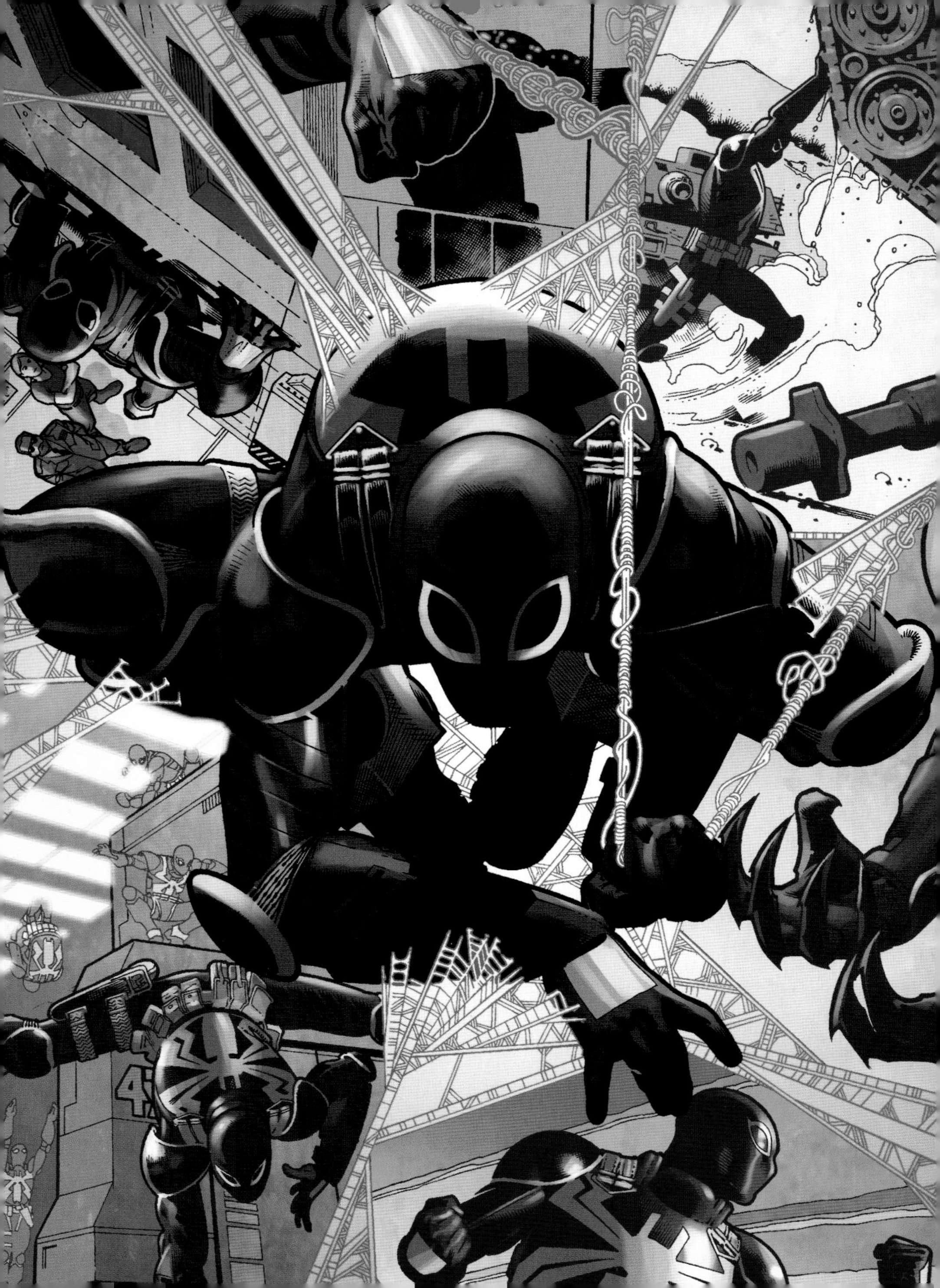

DON'T LET YOUR PAST DEFINE YOU

The ability to look back at regrets allows you to look ahead toward redemption. Case in point: Eugene "Flash" Thompson, Peter Parker's perpetual antagonist, seems almost irredeemable, but everyone loves a comeback. Flash's story starts when he bullies Peter relentlessly in high school. Ironically, he idolizes Spider-Man, not knowing the Web-Head's true identity.

Then, inspired by his favorite hero and craving a sense of direction, Flash decides to redeem himself by joining the army. He is badly injured in combat, losing his legs, then bonds with the amorphous organism Venom. Through this transformation, Flash learns to control his emotions while taming the parasitic symbiote. Newly empowered as Agent Venom, he sees his past behavior anew. He decides to change his narrative again, and so begins a life as a hero. Flash goes from selfish to selfless, using his new abilities to right wrongs.

We all do things we regret. Our regrettable things may vary in degree, but the feeling of shame or guilt is always there. Yet it doesn't mean we can't move forward. We can attempt to wrestle control of our own inner symbiote by taking responsibility for our past actions. Asking forgiveness from yourself and others is difficult but worth it. Make your distant past just that: distant. And create a new path forward for yourself. After all, if Flash Thompson can change, *anyone* can.

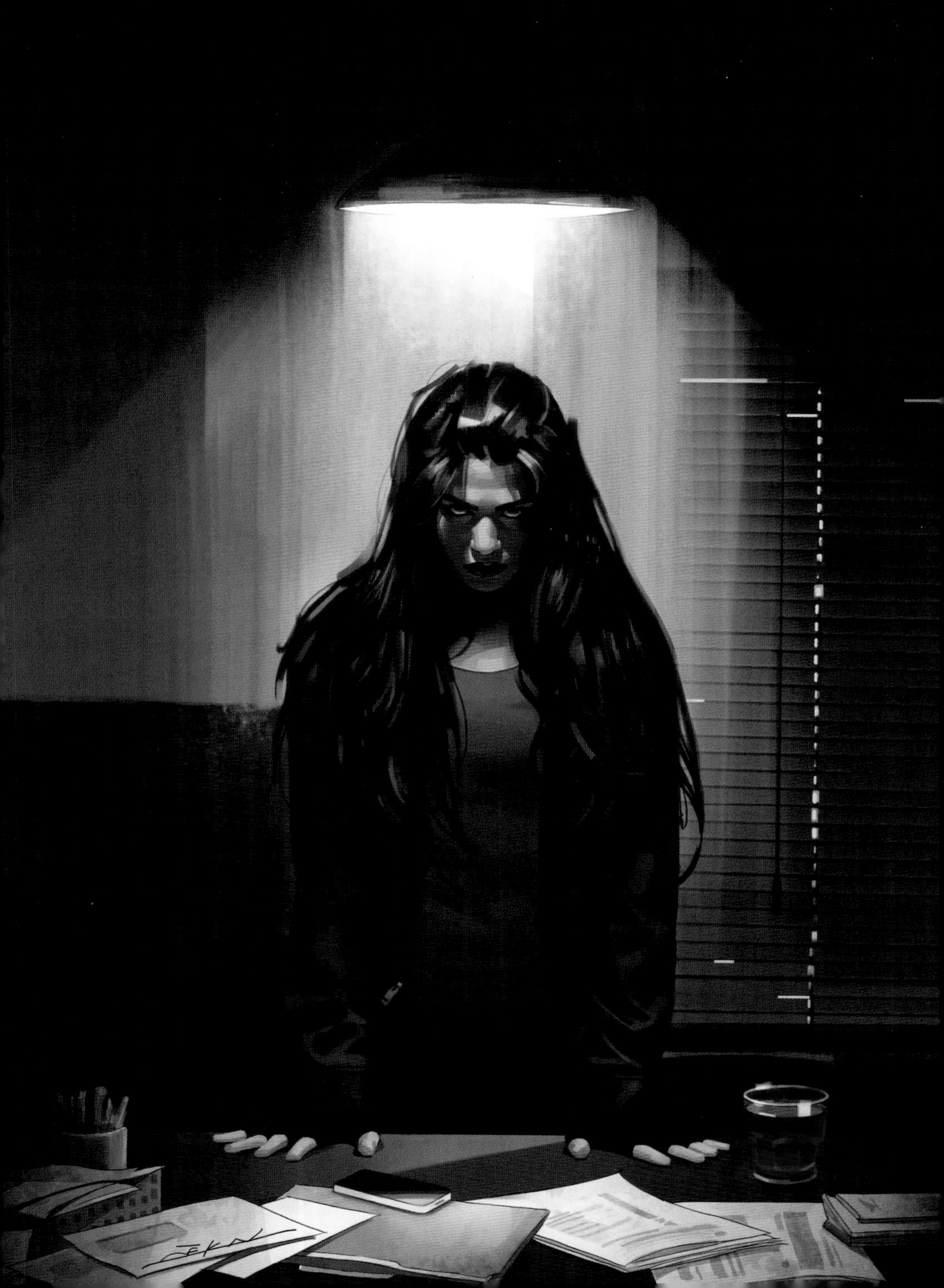

EMPOWER YOURSELF

Finding the strength within yourself is a journey. After all, it's hard enough to figure out who you are and your place in the world, never mind having someone mind-control your every move. A private investigator dealing with her own trauma, Jessica Jones isn't your regular super hero, and it's not because of her lack of costume. Gaining her powers after a car accident, she develops superhuman strength and even the ability to fly. Jessica's new powers would be an asset to any team, but her real talent is her ability to harness her inner strength.

Able to bend others to his will, super villain Zebediah Killgrave—also known as the Purple Man—uses his persuasive powers to subject Jessica to eight months of mental and physical abuse. Once she finally breaks free from his spell, she begins to recover from the pain of that situation, but it never truly leaves her. Still, she soldiers on and fights for others who don't have a voice. Jessica's hardships are something she will always have to deal with, but she refuses to let her trauma define her.

Working through painful memories takes time—you don't wake up one day completely healed. And that's okay. Jessica may have superhuman strength, but her struggles are relatable to anyone who needs to galvanize their own courage from within. When you start your journey to recovery, tap into your inner Jessica Jones. What will make you whole? Is it self-compassion or being your own Defender? More time? Or all of the above? Once you discover the answer, you'll find yourself empowered.

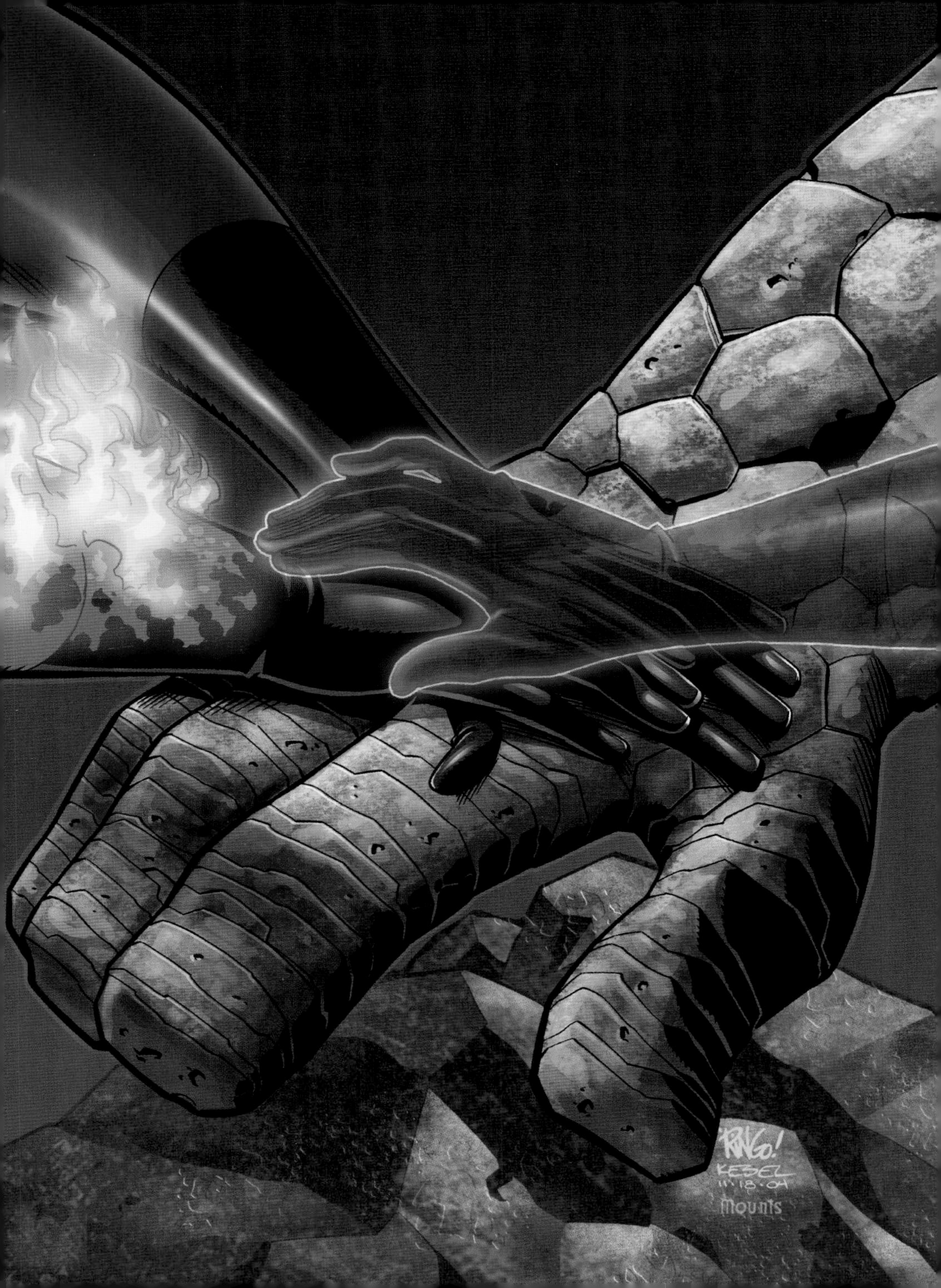
RINGO!
KESEL
11·18·04
Mounts

MAINTAIN RELATIONSHIPS

Keeping a family together is no easy task. It takes communication and understanding—and having super-stretchy arms can help. Being the first family of the Marvel Universe is quite a mantle to uphold, but if anyone can do it, it's Reed Richards; Sue Storm; her brother, Johnny; and Ben Grimm. After an experimental space flight exposes them to cosmic radiation that gives them strange new abilities, they take on the names Mister Fantastic, the Invisible Woman, the Human Torch, and the Thing to form the Fantastic Four.

Despite their new powers, the foursome can't hide their all-too-human vulnerabilities. For example, as the Thing, Ben's hot temper can't change the fact that his body is now in an unalterable rock-like form. Reed feels responsible for his best friend's tragedy, and the pain of this blame is often behind Reed's and Ben's misunderstandings and conflicts. Ben ultimately forgives him because it's their communication that always brings the team back together—even when it involves yelling. Through good times and bad, small squabbles and galactic catastrophes, they continue to love and support one another.

Whether it's your birth family or a chosen crew, maintaining connections is all about communication. Listening to all sides of a situation and trying to keep a team together can be hard, but in the end it's worth finding common ground and overcoming your differences, whether you're saving the world from a Kree invasion or just trying to maintain the peace at Thanksgiving.

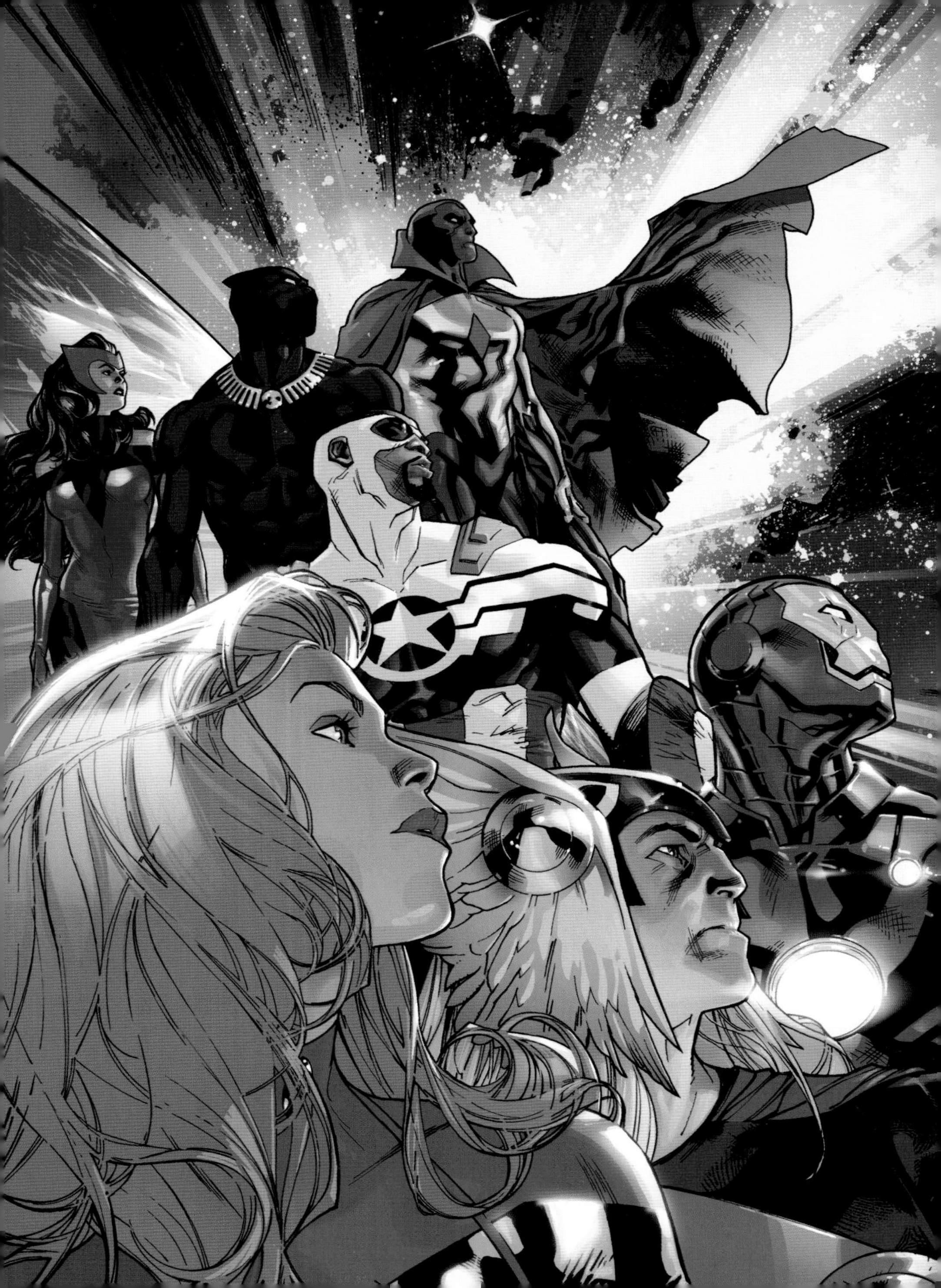

TEAMWORK MAKES THE DREAM WORK

Assemble to get the job done. There have been many team-ups throughout Marvel history, from Alpha Flight to the X-Men, the Fantastic Four to the Inhumans, but it's the Avengers who continue to be one of the most iconic. The Avengers' core belief of being a powerful force for fighting injustice is the glue that keeps them together.

The team lineup has changed over the years since the original roster of Iron Man, Thor, Ant-Man, and the Wasp assembled to defend the Hulk against the one and only Loki. This beginning led to many adventures fighting against the evilest of villains. What has kept the Avengers together at their core is unity—their solid belief in doing the right thing, together.

As Tony Stark can attest, keeping a team of big personalities together is difficult. Sometimes a good Hulk-smash feels like the only real solution to a conflict, but that's why you have teammates: to handle things that you can't tackle alone. Everyone has their own skillset, and combining those talents for a common goal is when the magic happens. Bringing together Odin-strength with tiny-but-mighty ant-abilities doesn't seem like a likely pairing, but it's that dichotomy that forms the synergy for a perfect team. Sure, sometimes even Earth's Mightiest Heroes have trouble staying on task, but keeping your crew together for the common good will always be a win.

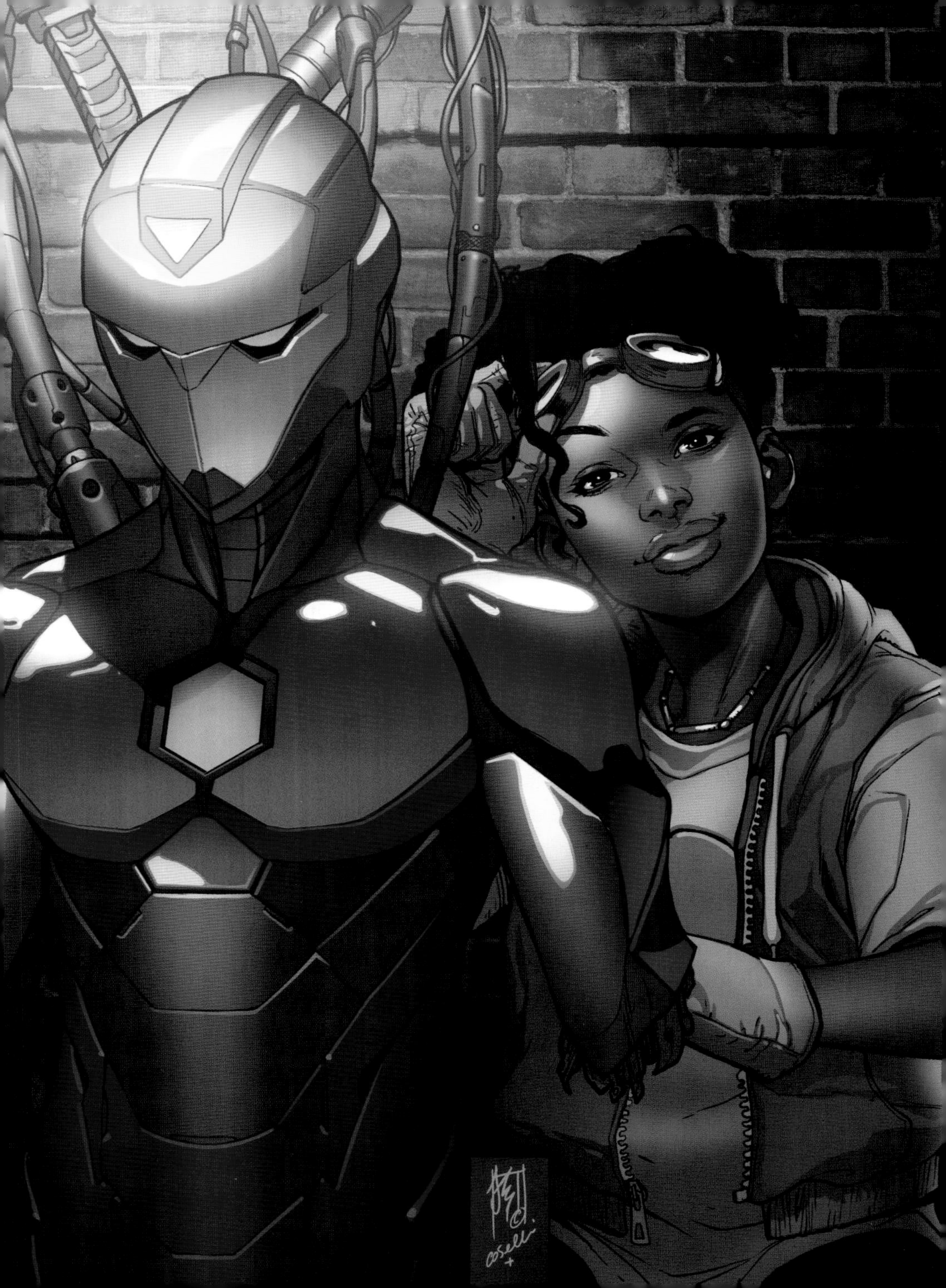

FOLLOW YOUR HEART

Feeling apprehensive about a situation? Just follow your heart. Actually, an arc reactor will do, plus it will give you highly detailed statistics, as it does for young super-genius Riri Williams, who had to take a huge leap of faith to become the hero she always wanted to be.

While Riri lacks powers, her super-intelligence makes her one of the smartest people in the world. Riri has always idolized Tony Stark, even going so far as to build her own advanced armor based on Iron Man's suit. When she takes on the moniker Ironheart and uses her intellect to fight crime, Tony Stark's encouragement sets aside any doubts she has of becoming a true hero. So when she learns that Tony Stark has died, Riri is devastated and feels helpless without her mentor. But she trusts what her heart tells her to do, digs deep, and finds the confidence to follow in his footsteps and move forward.

Taking a pause to reassess things is a good plan of attack when you're feeling uncomfortable, whether it's going to a new school or planning a big presentation. Be the Tony Stark to your Riri, and look at yourself as your mentor would. Listen to your own advice—do what your heart tells you. Uncertainty can feel like jumping off a ledge without repulsors, but once you trust your own instincts, you'll realize that you can let go of the guardrails and believe in yourself.

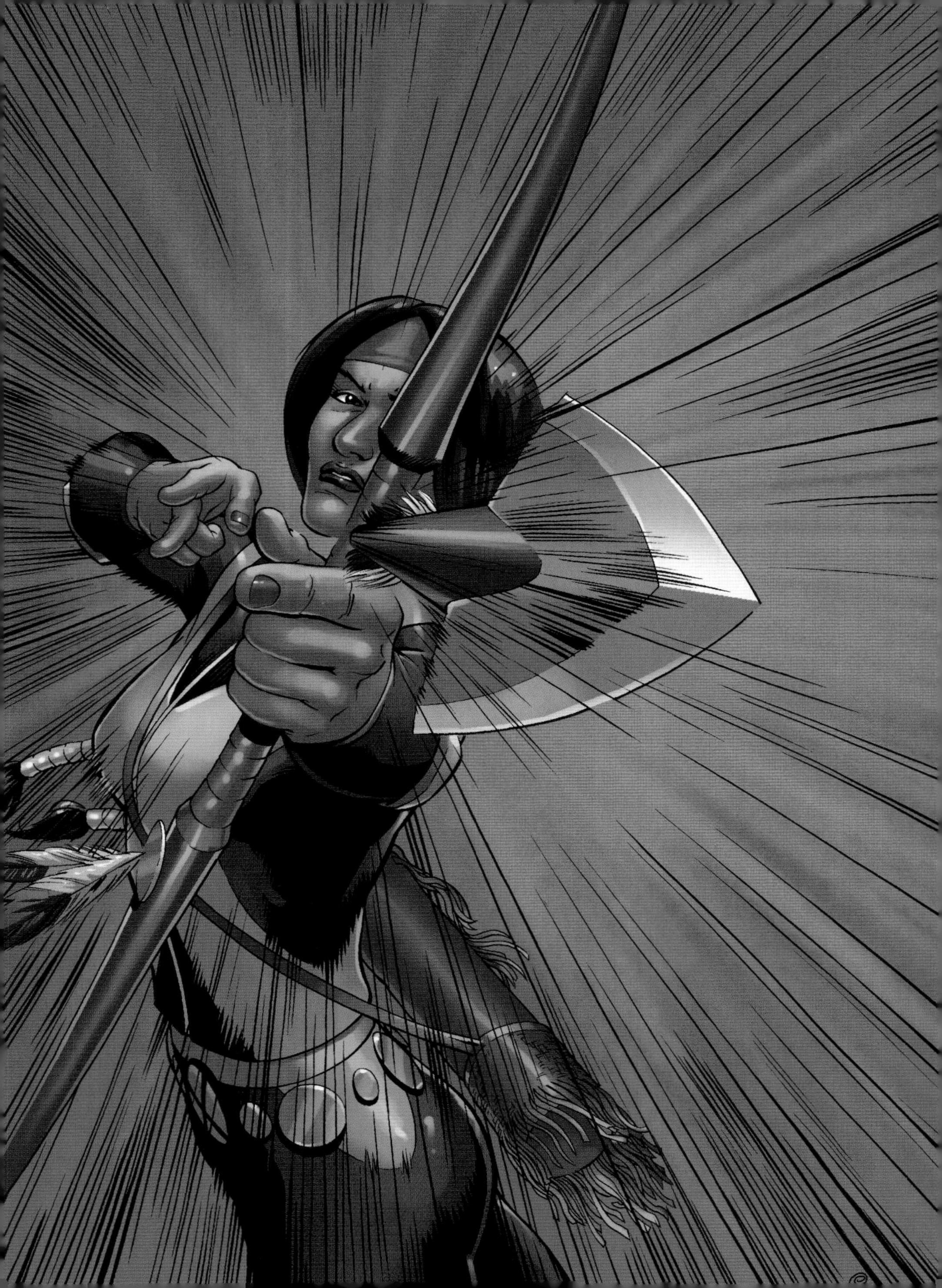

BE TRUE TO YOURSELF

Working with a team doesn't mean you have to lose your identity. Anchored by her heritage, Danielle "Dani" Moonstar has gone by many names. A member of the Cheyenne Nation, she's been known as Moonstar, Psyche, and Mirage, and she was also a Valkyrie. Carrying on the traditions and teachings of her grandfather Black Eagle is something that she carries with herself through every trial.

When Charles Xavier first recruits the New Mutants, he instructs them to wear official X-Men uniforms. Dani adorns the outfit with a symbol of her Native heritage and stands firm in the face of criticism. Xavier could force her to comply, but instead he listens as Dani explains that she needs to honor her heritage—doing anything less would strip away her individuality. Intelligent and fearless, Dani remains true to herself and what she stands for.

Your biggest assets and your unique point of view are what distinguish you from others. Dani stands on the shoulders of her ancestors and uses that vantage point as her guide through life. In the same way, be true to who you are and don't hide what you have to offer. When you're asked to conform, but the idea doesn't sit right with you, assert your beliefs. Stand up for yourself when it feels right, and like Dani, you can lead by example.

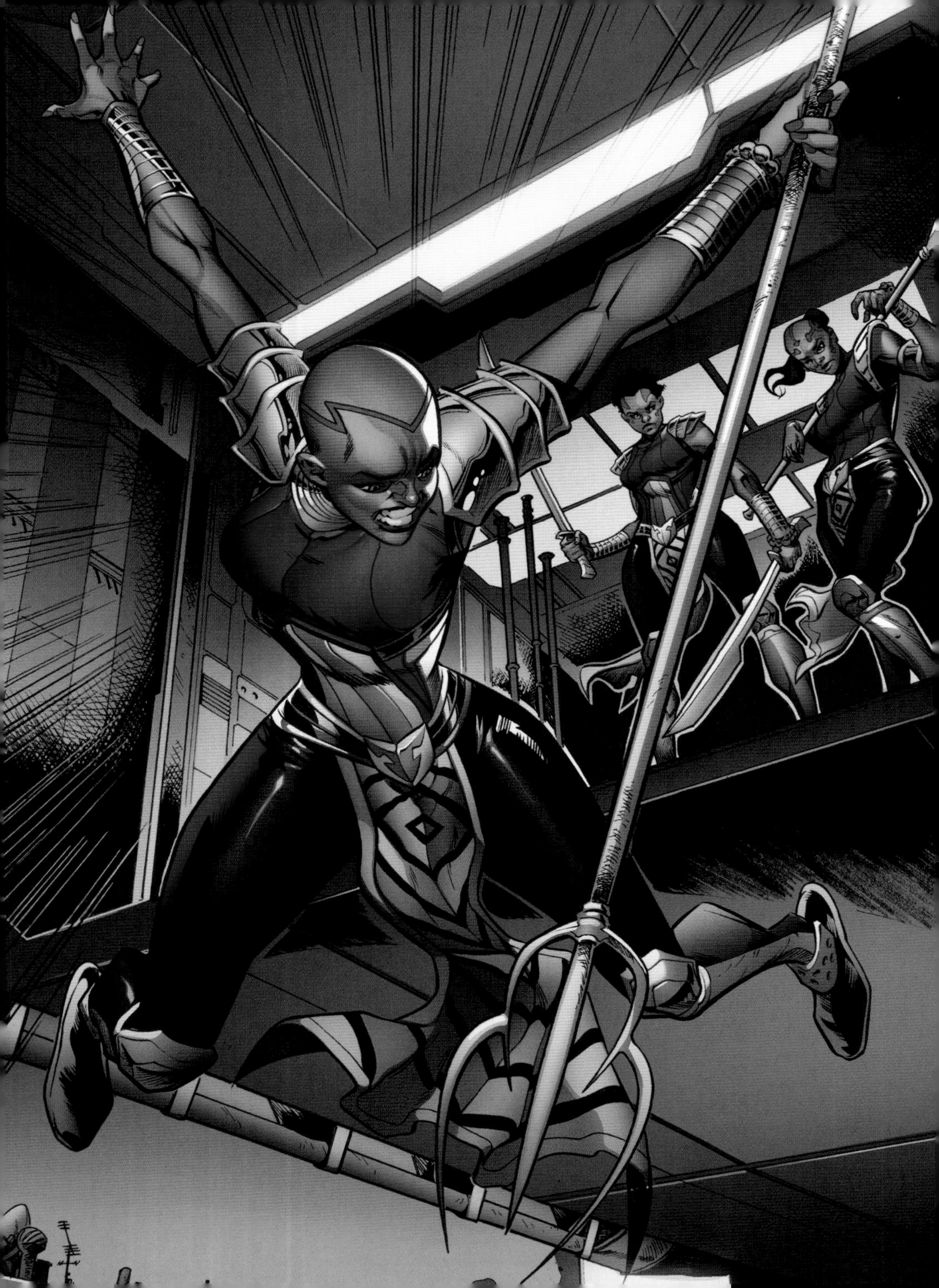

PROTECT OTHERS

Using your abilities to protect others is the most noble of causes. The Dora Milaje are a prime example of sacrificing for something larger than yourself. Brought together to serve the Black Panther, the Dora Milaje are a collective of daughters assembled from the tribes of Wakanda. As T'Challa's bodyguards, their goal is to protect and defend their king under any and all circumstances. They use their fighting skills as well as their intellect, aided by Wakandan technology, wearing vibranium armor and utilizing kimoyo beads to communicate. The Dora know they are stronger together and are a force to be reckoned with.

With ranks that number over five hundred strong, these fierce warriors have a powerful sense of loyalty to their king and their homeland. Fueled by their noble, intense pride and passion, the Dora Milaje have fought everyone from Killmonger to Doctor Doom in the name of Wakanda. In addition to having their own families to protect, they put their lives on the line for the greater good. These women will stop at nothing to maintain peace and fight for justice.

Don't let injustices stand. The Dora have a village mentality and protect others before themselves. You can apply this same idea to your own life, in ways as big as fighting for a cause larger than your own, or as simple as standing up for the little guy. The decision may be difficult, but the reward is knowing you've protected others who may not have the strength to do it themselves. Defending what's right is the most heroic thing a person can do.

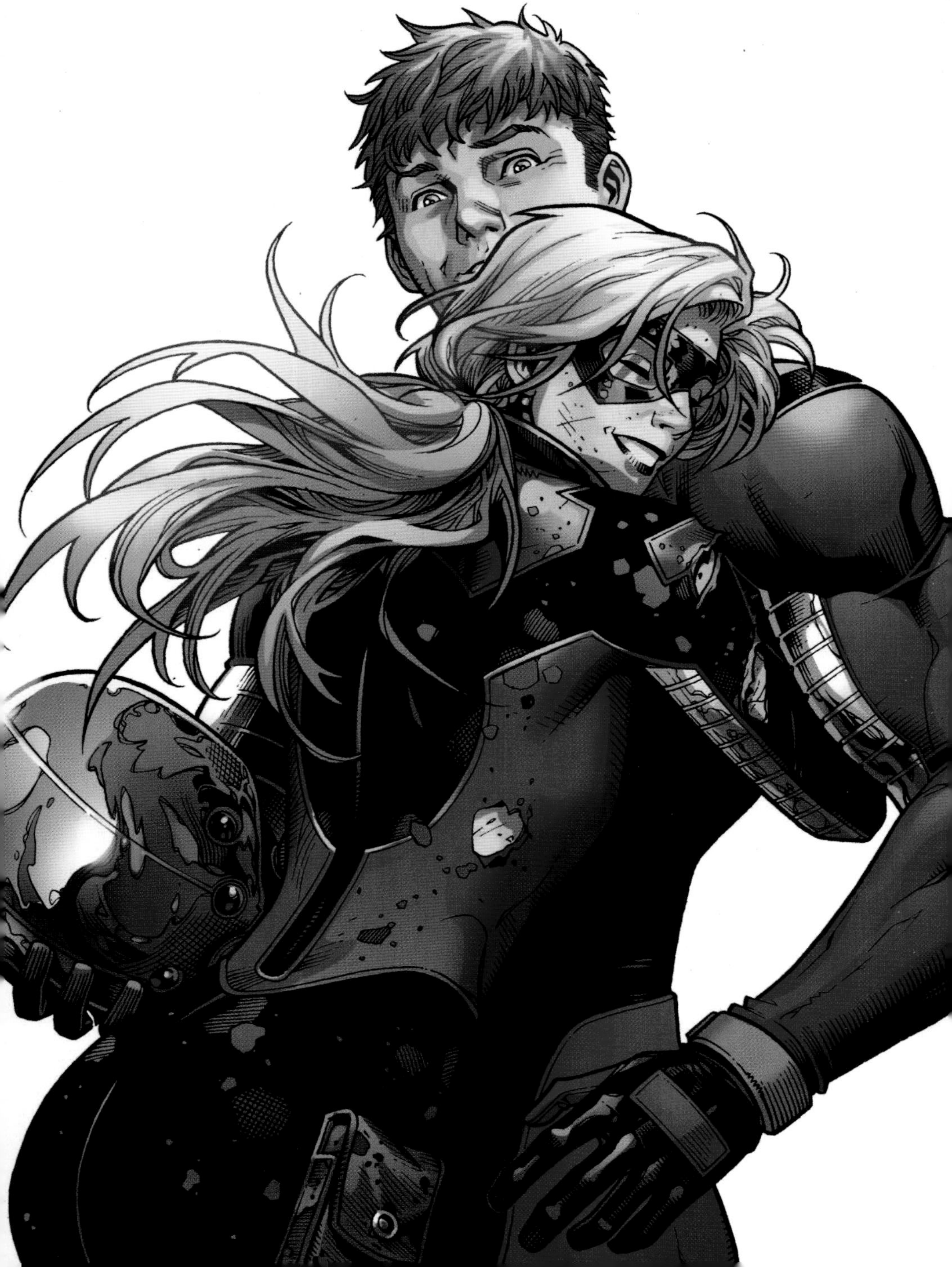

NO PROBLEM IS
TOO SMALL

For Scott Lang, size matters. When it comes to a super hero's personal issues, problems can be as big as a cosmic entity devouring planets or as small as forgetting where you put the keys to the Fantasti-Car. As Ant-Man, Scott deals with otherworldly threats while also trying to live like a normal guy trying to do his best. Being Cassie's father is his most important role, and when she needs him, he's always there for her. When Cassie fell ill and her surgeon was kidnapped, Scott returned to a life of crime to save her. Dad-life is his motivation, and he'll drop everything to make sure his daughter is safe.

Eventually, Scott and Cassie work together, with Cassie taking on the mantle of Stinger. (If being a crimefighting duo isn't enough pressure, imagine having to do this with your child. One: Focus on the villains. Two: Also try to be a good parental example.) It's true that any work situation with a parent and child is going to create some resistance on the latter's part. And indeed, Cassie, wanting freedom from her dad, wishes to be her own hero on her own terms. Instead, she and her dad work out their small issues to tackle bigger problems like defeating an evil egg-headed scientist. They ultimately develop a respect for each other that is beyond dad–daughter love—and they turn out to be a great team.

When you're dealing with larger issues in life, it's easy to dismiss small problems as unimportant. But those little things need to be taken care of too. Ignoring a leaky faucet can lead to a flooded kitchen. Letting a small disagreement fester can lead to a broken relationship. Stealing a super suit—well, that can lead to your becoming a big hero! (Or a small one.) Scott was able to keep larger issues at bay by working through smaller hurdles with Cassie. When you tackle your tiniest of problems, it's astonishingly huge what you can accomplish.

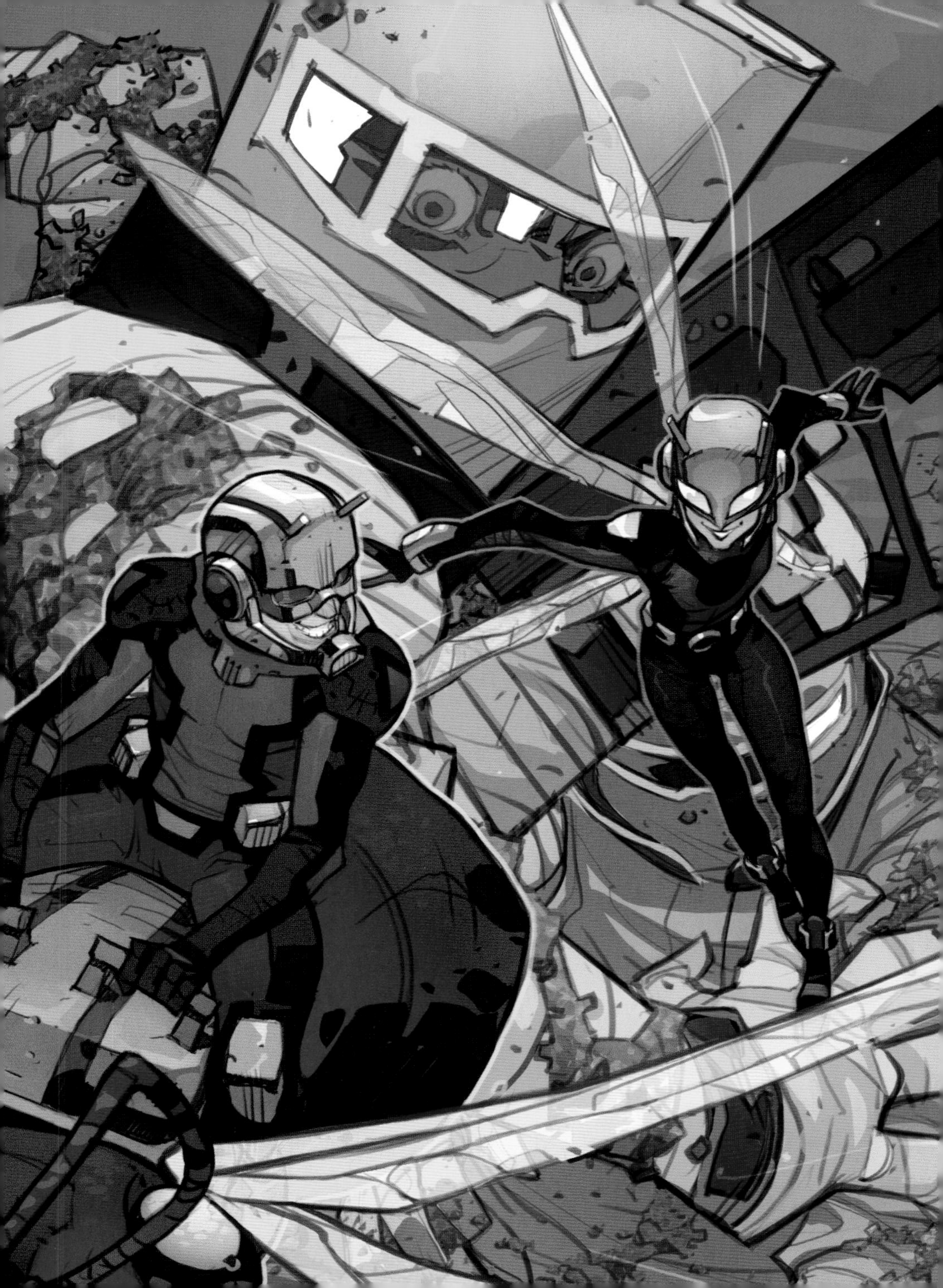

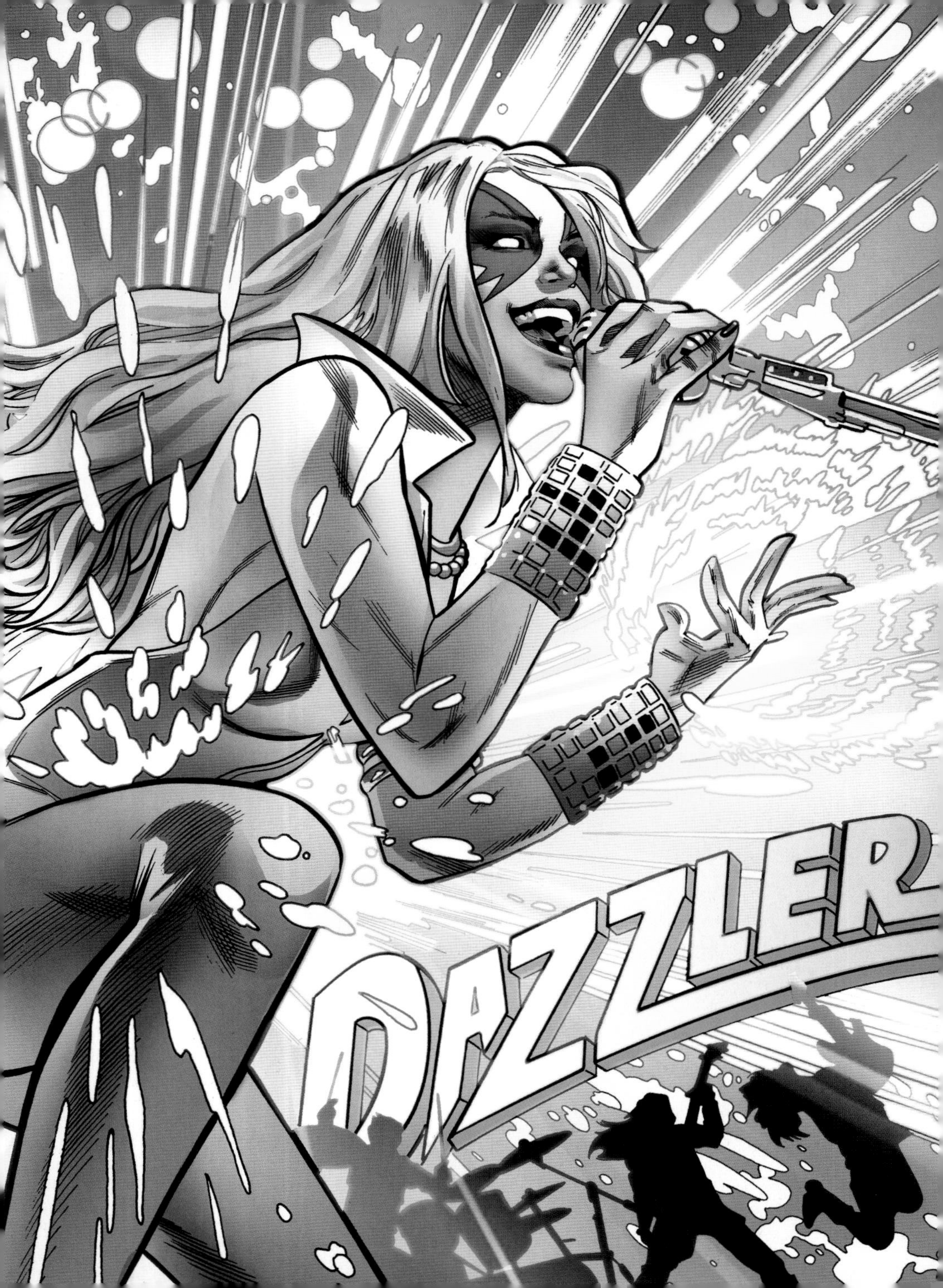
DAZZLER

SHINE BRIGHT

Don't dim your talents to make others feel more comfortable. Alison Blaire never wanted to follow in her father's footsteps of being a lawyer, nor did she want to be a hero once she discovered her mutant powers. All she wanted to do on stage was sing. Yet when her powers manifested as blinding light during a performance, she realized she had more than one calling.

A true shining star, Dazzler loves the spotlight, but mostly just when she's performing. As much as she tries to stay away from super hero duty, she always finds her way back to it. A powerful teammate—often with Beast and Johnny Storm—and a valued confidante, Dazzler has a way of standing out. As one of the most potent members of the X-Men, Dazzler's true talent is her drive to do what she loves to make herself happy.

Never let your own light be dimmed. Putting your own happiness goals first doesn't mean you're selfish—it's about setting boundaries so you have the space to nurture what makes you the best in what you love to do. Whether at work or in a social situation, if you aren't being given the platform to shine, channel your inner Dazzler. Find your stage, shine bright, and be proud of your accomplishments.

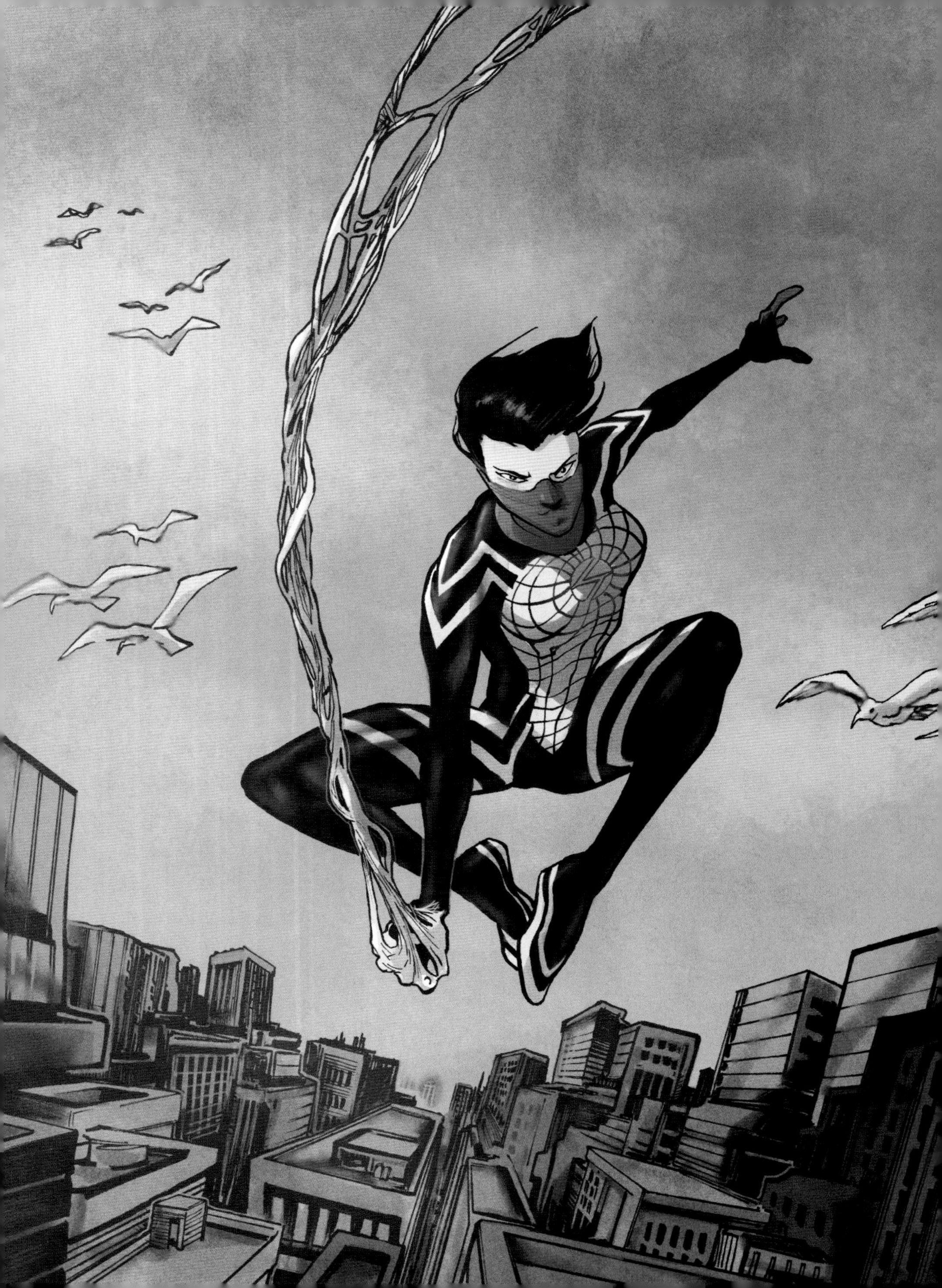

KEEP GOING

When you've reached rock bottom, keep swinging. Korean American Cindy Moon's super-origin is similar to that of another well-known arachnid-themed hero: not only was she Peter Parker's classmate, she also was bitten by the same radioactive spider. If that wasn't a big enough life change, she was then held captive in a bunker for ten years to hide her powers from totem predators. After training in hiding, she was eventually freed by none other than Peter himself.

Taking on the moniker of Silk, Cindy helps other multiversal spider-heroes while trying to regain all that she lost during her imprisonment. Then, as if a decade of captivity wasn't bad enough, Silk loses her powers during the Spider-Verse conflict and feels doubt and anxiety about her sense of self. These difficulties are setbacks for Cindy, but by joining teams like Agents of Atlas and forming the Order of the Web, she finds purpose, which gives her the strength to carry on.

When life beats you down, you might feel like there's no way out. But try putting yourself in Cindy Moon's shoes: ten years alone in a bunker could've been Cindy's downfall, but she didn't let it deter her from taking back her life. Even if you don't have a multiversal spider-army to turn to, it's possible to set your sights on overcoming obstacles on your own terms—and eventually get back into the swing of things.

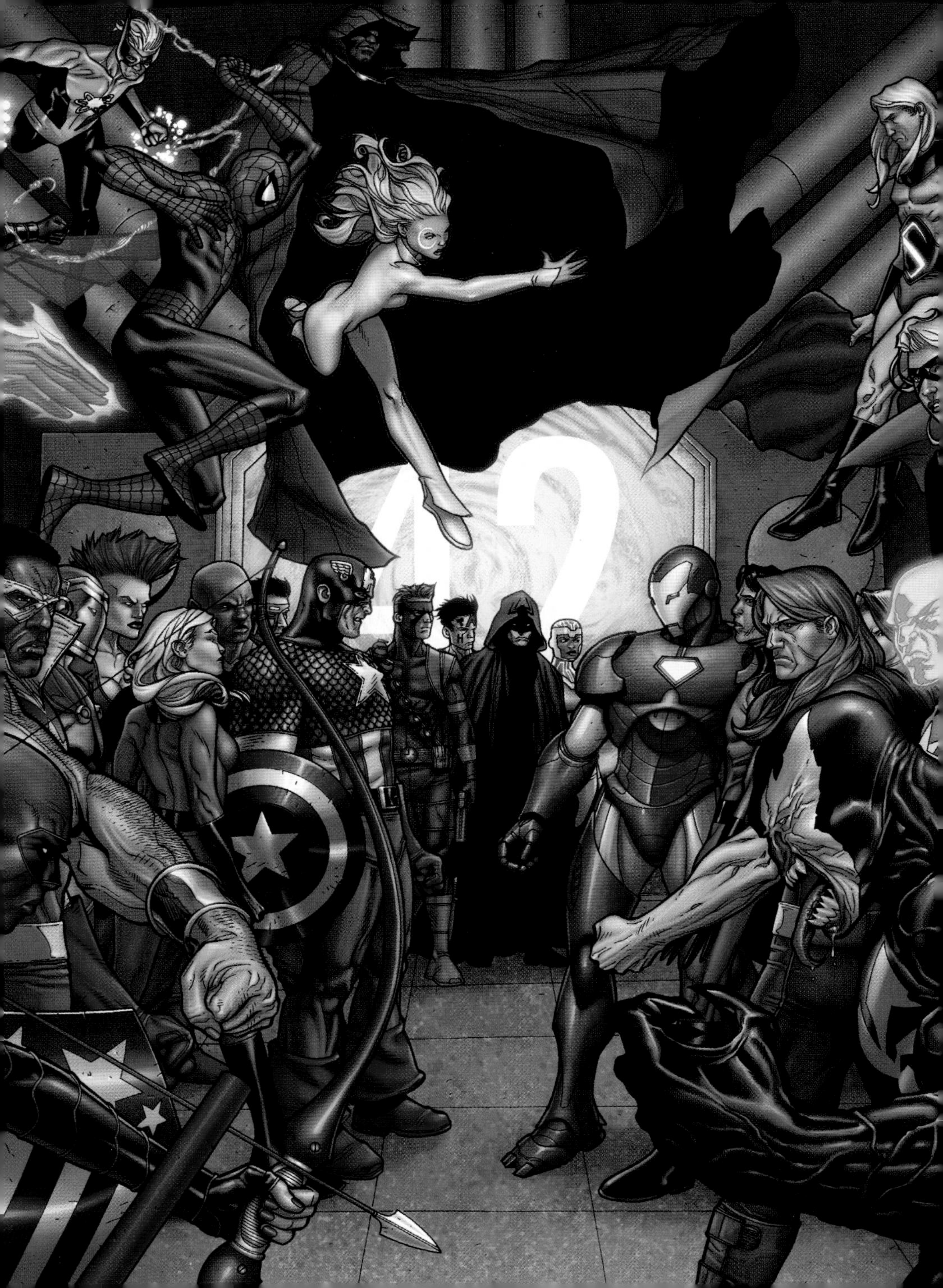
42

RESPECT ABOVE ALL ELSE

Fight with honor. Lead with respect. After being rejected by the army, Steve Rogers was given a second chance to fight for his country when offered the Super-Soldier Serum. Gaining power and strength was a new adventure in which he took on threats as a solo super hero and later as leader of the Avengers. Even with these new superior stats, Steve remained a man of integrity through and through.

Cap's belief in justice and fighting for what's right may motivate him, but respect is what keeps him humble. When he starts a Civil War between heroes, throughout all the battling both physical and emotional, Steve maintains his admiration for every member on both sides of the fight. Even when Cap holds an opposing viewpoint, he keeps his former-teammates-turned-foes in high esteem.

When Steve decides to pass on the mantle to Sam Wilson, he does so knowing he chose a man with aligned beliefs who will lead with his heart. His respect for Sam is well earned and Cap knows he is making the right decision.

When you're caught in a tough situation, it's easy to forget that your enemy has their own beliefs they are also fighting for. So, put down your defensive vibranium shield and keep in mind that your opponent deserves to have their voice heard as well, even if their point of view is not your own. Try to see your adversary through their eyes and give them the respect they deserve, even if their viewpoint isn't your own.

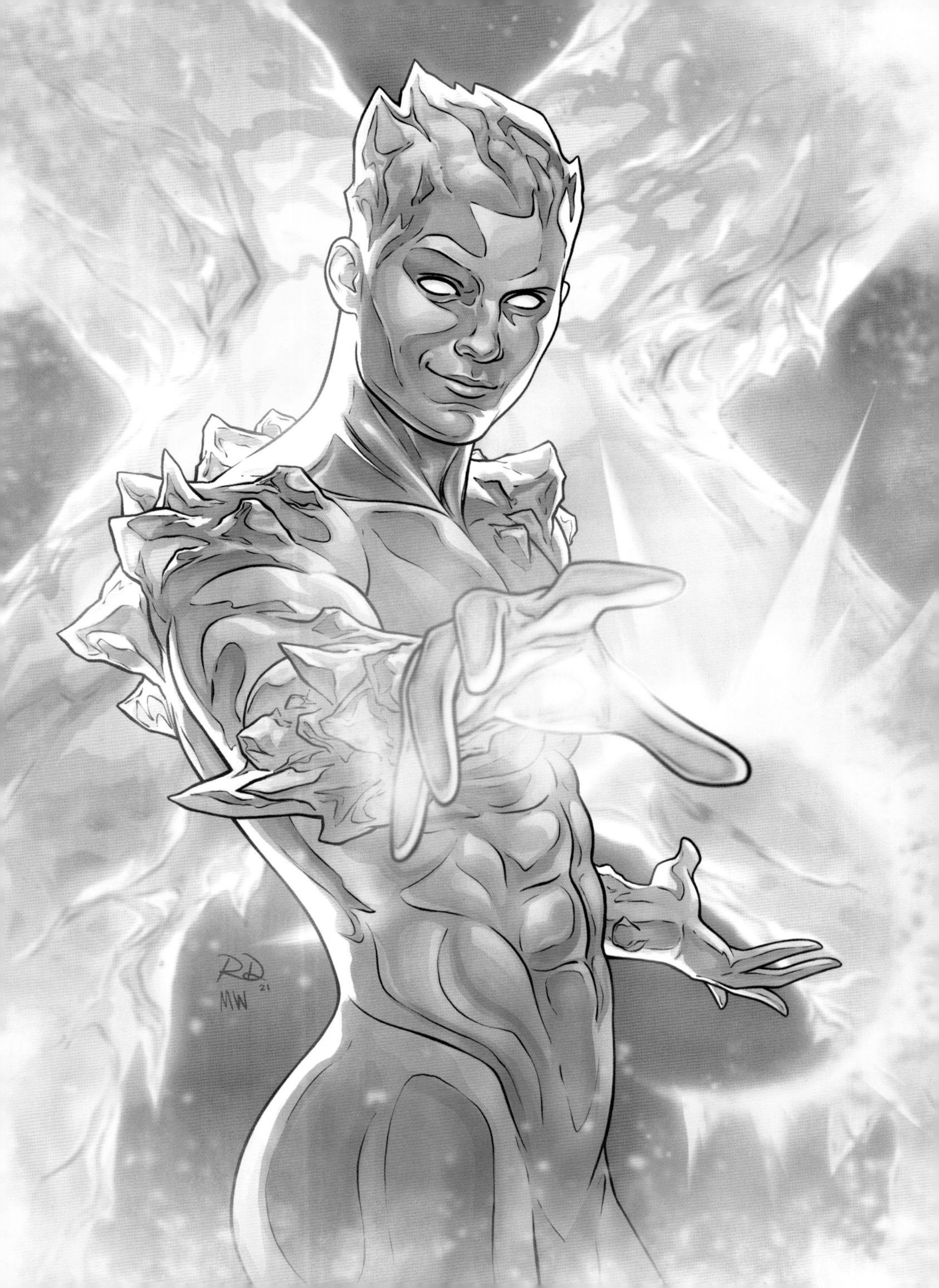

BE YOU, FOR YOU

Bobby Drake knows how to keep his cool. Literally. Nevertheless, even Iceman, born with the power to control cold and ice, can let his core melt down to his true self. Whether being confronted by his future self, or giving an interview after saving the world, Bobby is able to reflect and realize that the best way to become a better leader is to be himself.

Through a series of events and (what else?) time travel, young Bobby, with Jean Grey by his side, confronts his older self and learns that he had a fear of coming out and being persecuted for being gay. Jean tells him that by accepting himself and his sexual identity, he will not only be a better X-Man but also, by his example, the leader the team most needs.

After stopping a solar storm alongside his old teammate Firestar, Iceman makes a statement to a reporter, asking the public to see him for who he is:

I don't want anybody to thank me for what my friends and I did today. That's never why we do it, but if you want to do me one solid, see me for who I am.

A mutant. A gay man.

I know that's two strikes with a bunch of the folks I helped save today, and I'll be honest . . . even after everything I've been through, it still hurts. I can change my body. I can look like your "normal." Lately, I've been wearing my ice because I'm proud of who I am, and I'm doing it for all the mutants who can't look like humans and don't want to. Maybe I can save some young mutants and humans some time and some grief. Don't wait to be who you are, and don't be ashamed of that person.

Coming to terms with your true self takes time—and can be frustrating and terrifying—but it's time well spent. Accepting your authentic self can come with a joyous feeling of liberation. Even ice-cold Bobby Drake learned to wear his emotions on his sleeve and experience shared happiness. So, take heart: there will be doubts, there will be fears, but being yourself is ultimately the best thing for you.

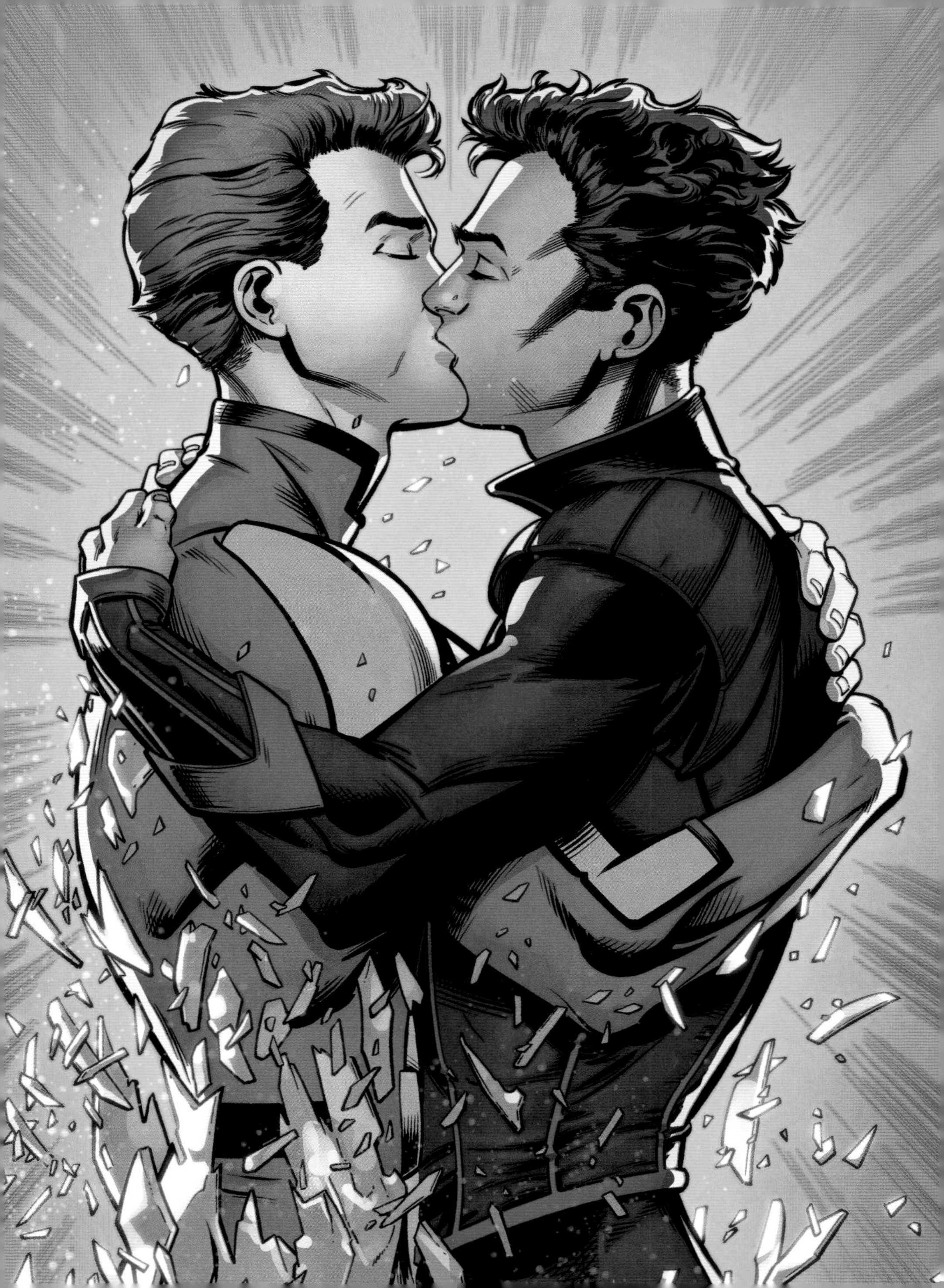

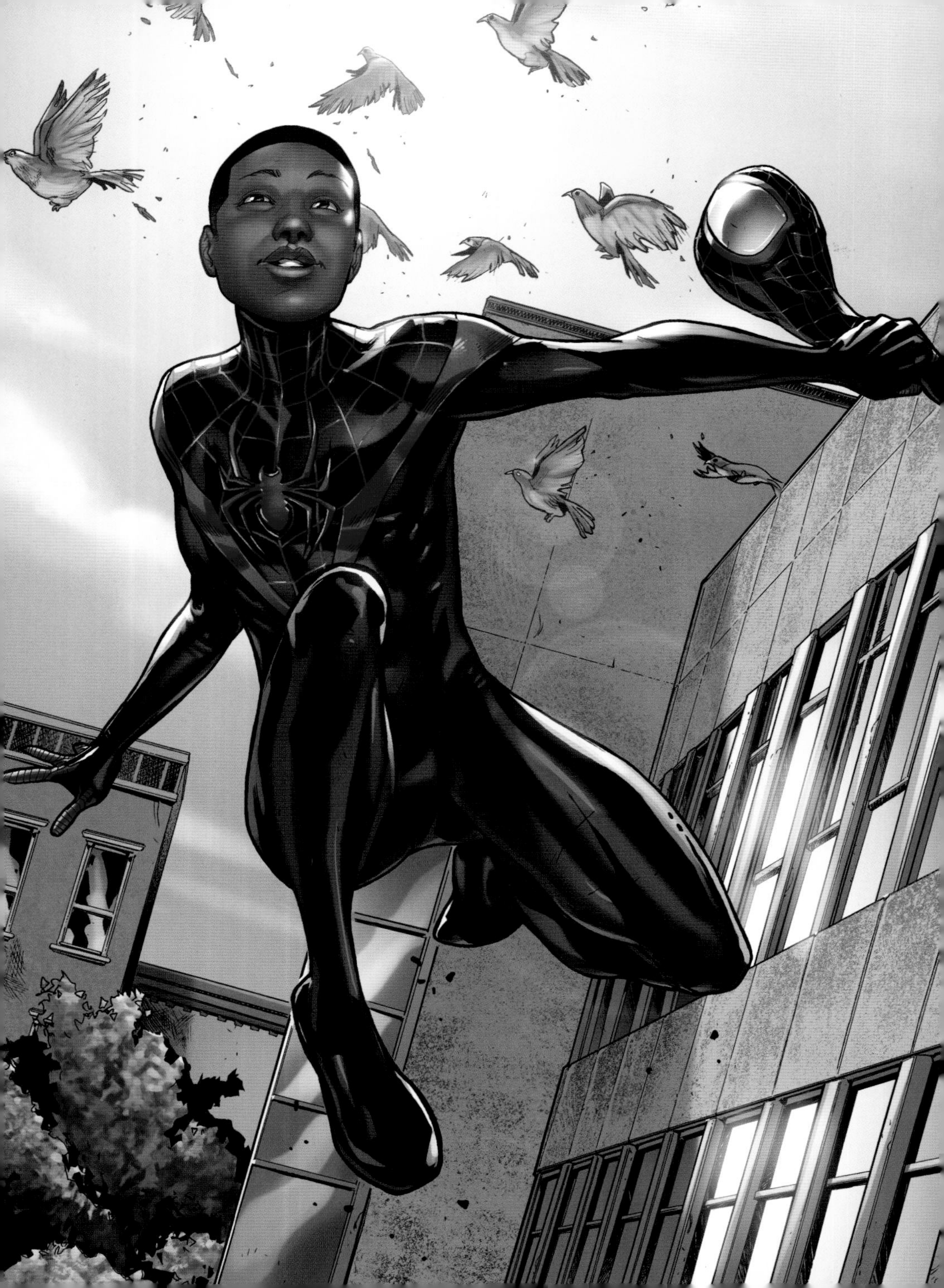

BE RESILIENT

Being able to dig deep into what matters to us is what allows us to swing back from adversity. Take, for example, the alternate reality of Earth-1610, where a young New York City teen is bitten by a genetically enhanced spider. When the Peter Parker of that dimension is killed, the teen—Miles Morales—is inspired to take up Spider-Man's fallen mantle.

Like Peter, Miles faces many challenges. His mom is accidentally killed in a scuffle with the symbiote Venom, and then his girlfriend turns out to be a Hydra agent. Sometimes his everyday life as a young teen is even more confounding than his life as Spider-Man. Yet through it all, Miles has to quickly learn to recover and rise back up.

Making difficult choices can be tough whether you're a seasoned hero or a newly minted one like Miles. And tenacity doesn't come easily to most; not everyone automatically has the kind of super-hero-level resiliency that allows them to climb right back up walls after getting knocked down. Motivation is key. Miles's faith in humanity helps him confirm what he's fighting for—a better world for all. Find a way to dig deep into what motivates you. Then let it fuel your journey back to square one, and keep fighting the good fight.

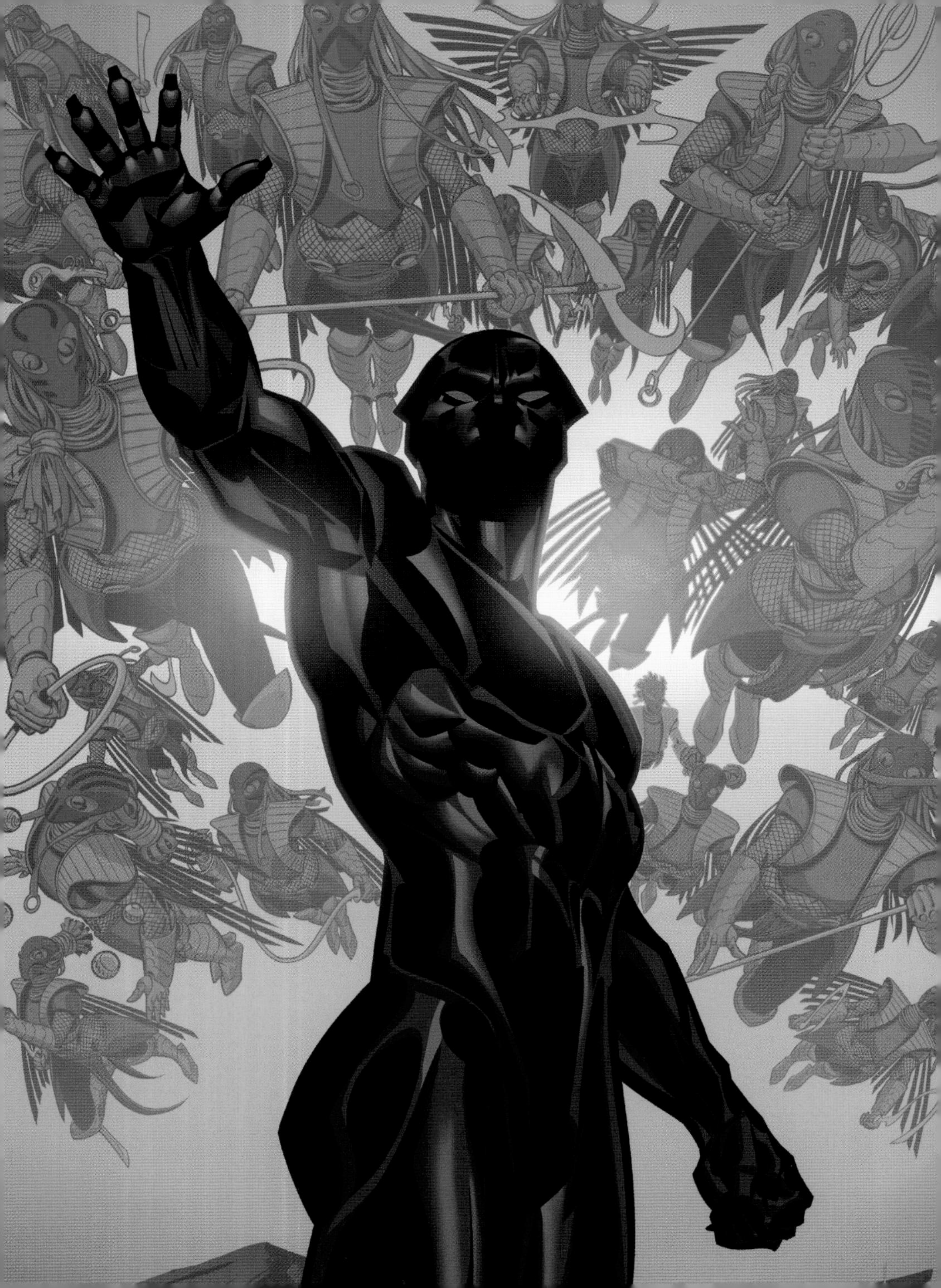

STEP INTO YOUR DESTINY

Accept your readiness, and lean on your preparedness. Stepping into a role you're destined for can be daunting. Case in point: T'Challa knows his obligation is to eventually take over for his father, T'Chaka, as both the king of Wakanda and the next Black Panther, but he does not expect it to be so soon. When T'Chaka meets an untimely death at the hands of Baron Zemo, T'Challa is thrust into the role of king. Destined and prepared for it as he was, but feeling both unready and angry at his father's passing, he is reluctant to sit on the throne, and instead is hell-bent on revenge.

Undergoing a long journey away from Wakanda and working through his sorrow and pain, T'Challa comes to accept that his homeland will always be foremost in his heart. Further, his confidence is boosted when he teams up with Captain America to stop a man posing as Baron Zemo and fight the Grim Reaper, thus becoming one of the Avengers. Eventually he reconciles his anger, accepts his destiny, and becomes the leader he was born to be.

Of course, ruling as the king of a vibranium-rich country isn't quite the same as leveling up at work or taking on big opportunities, but the stresses are similar. Are you good enough to take that step? Can you handle the pressure? These lingering questions can eat away at you. Getting out of your own head is the beginning: Tell yourself that you've been training to take on great responsibility, and now it's time to put that work to the test. Focus, believe in yourself, and trust that you're more than ready to take on whatever comes your way.

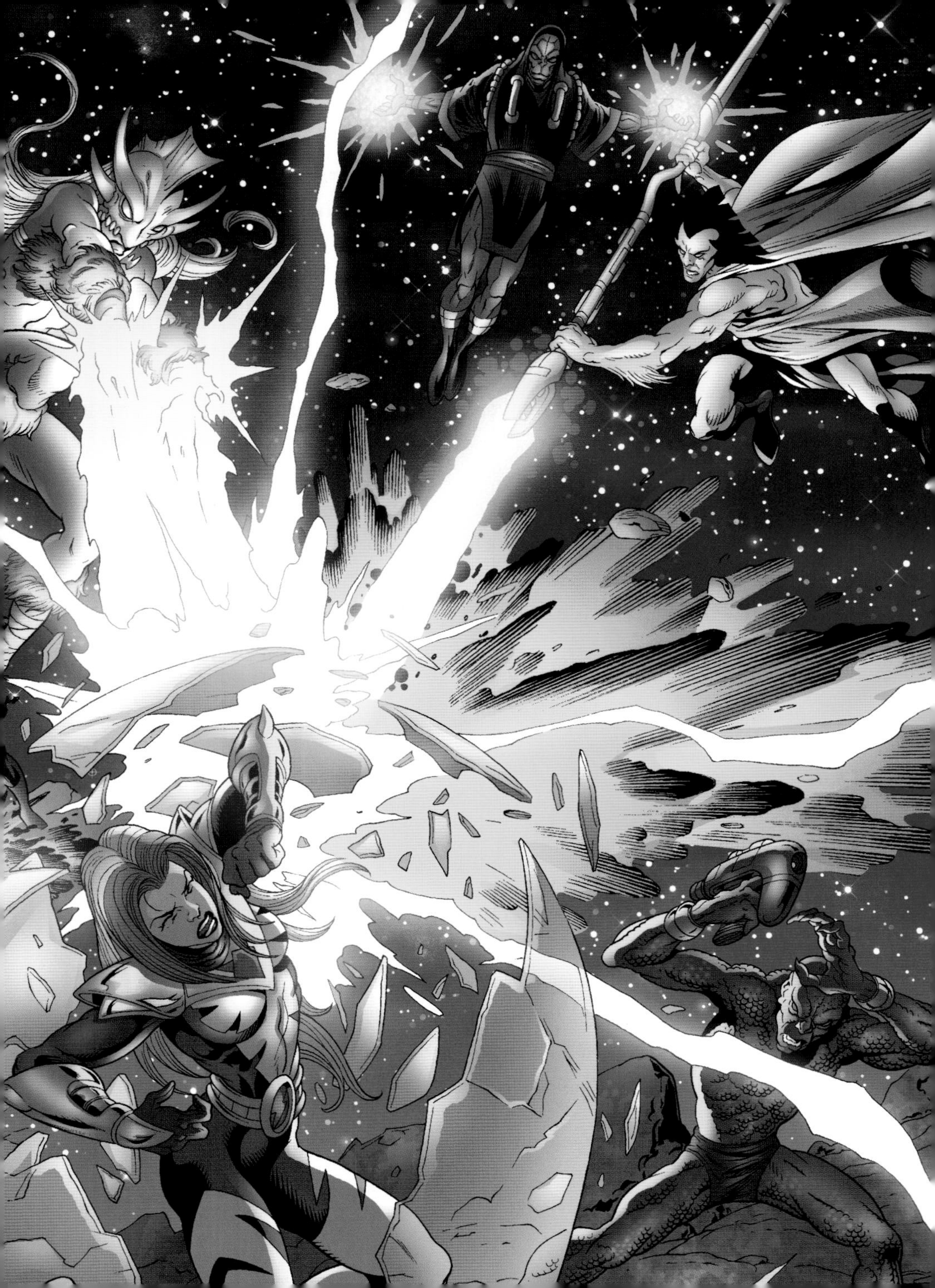

CHANGE YOUR NARRATIVE

Bad guys don't always have to be bad. Under the direction of Baron Zemo, former members of the Masters of Evil—Beetle, Fixer, Goliath, Moonstone, and Screaming Mimi—all pretend to be heroes . . . until they realize that they actually kind of like it. Switching up the narrative of their respective life journeys, they split from Zemo and call themselves the Thunderbolts. Hawkeye is the first of many leaders who take them under his wing and help them hone their skills.

And then, during the Civil War over the Superhuman Registration Act, a larger threat emerges—Grandmaster, who uses the Wellspring of Power to grant people all over the world enhanced abilities and is able to manipulate them through that power. The teams fighting for or against the Act join together to fight a common enemy. The Thunderbolts, along with their Thunderbolts Army of reformed villains, finally defeat Grandmaster . . . but then some of the Thunderbolts turn on the others. The team is at a crossroads, each of them tempted: they can choose to return to their evil ways or remain the heroes they know they can be. The Thunderbolts' lineup has changed a lot over the years, but those who committed to changing their narrative knew that being on the team offered a chance at redemption.

It's not easy to turn over a new leaf—much less continue along that journey, especially if you have a real-life evil league constantly trying to hold you back. Even with strong purpose, falling back to your old ways is possible. But if this happens, don't see it as a failure; instead, create a new narrative with yourself as the hero, even if you've made missteps you need to redeem.

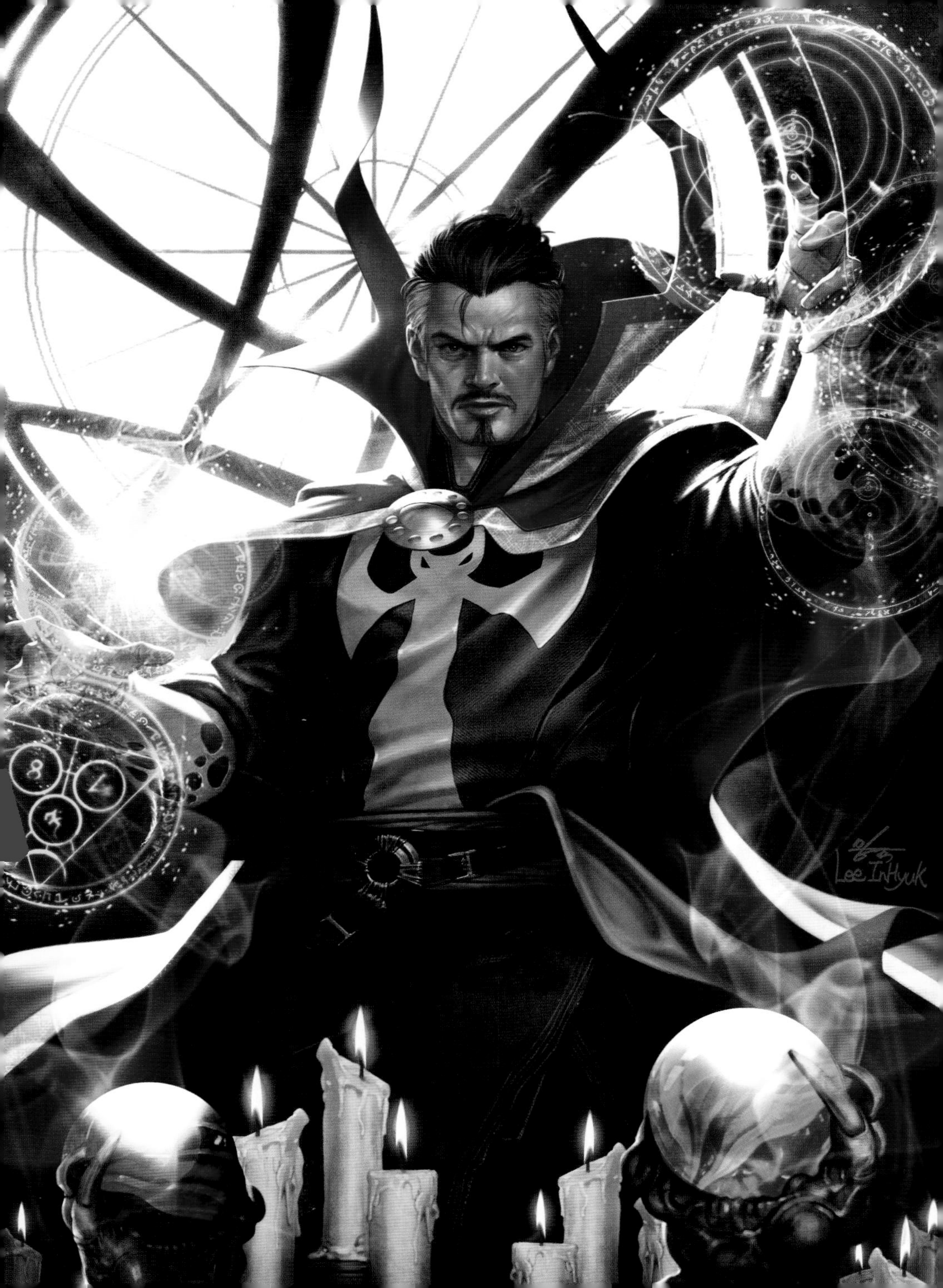
Lee InHyuk

STRIVE FOR ENLIGHTENMENT

In the darkest of timelines, it's hard to stay on the path toward making good choices. The well-respected yet arrogant neurosurgeon Doctor Stephen Strange has his life turned upside down one fateful night when a devastating car crash leaves him with nerve damage. His journey toward a clue leads him to the Ancient One, a mystic who offers him a glimpse into a larger universe. Learning from the Ancient One, Strange hones his skills in sorcery, eventually becoming a Master of the Mystic Arts.

Strange's prowess did not come without grave challenges, ones he strove to conquer at risk of failure and even death. He is eventually led into a dalliance in the Dark Dimension, which forces him to confront mortal enemies as well as his own insecurities. Time and again, Doctor Strange gains and loses the title of Sorcerer Supreme. As enlightened as he has become, he often struggles to choose between the light and dark paths.

As Doctor Strange shows us, there is no easy shortcut for walking through life, and no sure enlightenment at the end of the journey. The key can be in constantly searching, as Doctor Strange does, for answers to the unknown. When you face insurmountable challenges, rather than taking a "woe is me" attitude and shutting down, look at your problems with Doctor Strange's keen mind and open heart. It might give you a new perspective on how to tackle what's troubling you. And if things become overwhelming, use your own Sanctum Santorum for respite when you need to recuperate and refocus.

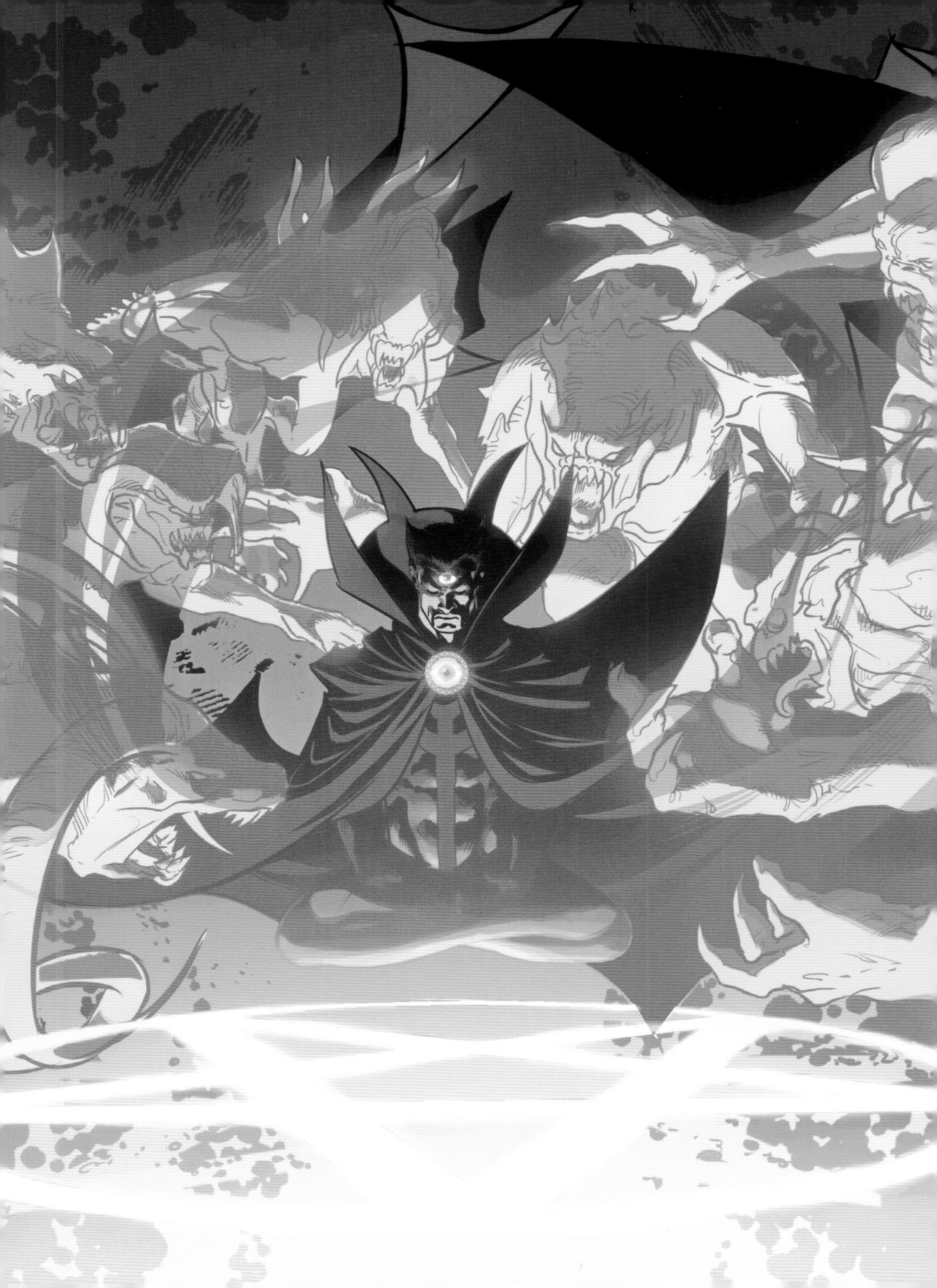

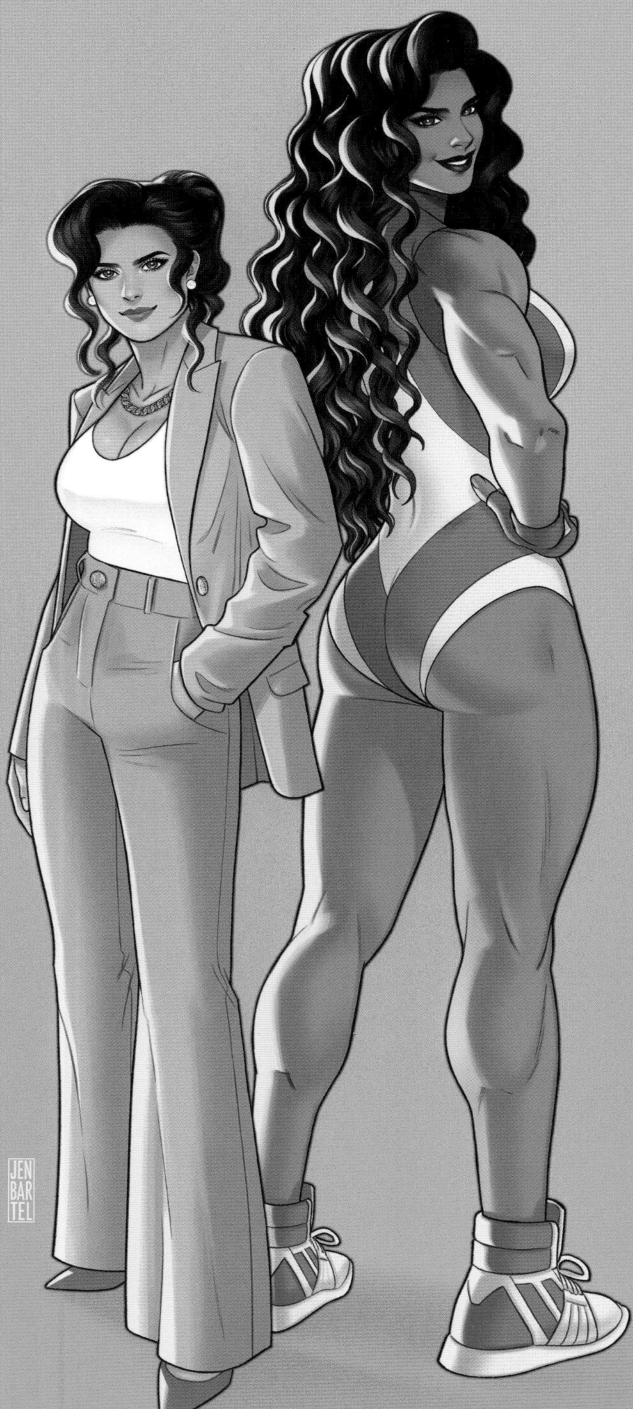
JEN BARTEL

BEING A HERO IS ABOUT MORE THAN STRENGTH

Jennifer Walters definitely knows what it takes to win a fight. One of the best defense attorneys in New York, she is also a 6'7", 700-pound cousin of the Hulk with his abilities—a commanding presence if there ever was one. What makes her different from her cousin is her ability to change personae at will. As She-Hulk, brute strength may be her first reaction, but she knows that rational thinking and determination can often be the best way to win a battle.

She-Hulk's emotional intelligence sets her apart, making her a good example of fighting the good fight on all levels. When Jennifer works as an attorney, she does so in her human form, not as She-Hulk. In the courtroom, she keeps her cool and handles stressful situations with ease. Jennifer's personality, humor, and sense of reason are her greatest strengths.

Making heroic decisions in life can be difficult, so finding a balance for yourself is key. Letting your emotions get the best of you and wanting to take matters into your own hands is an understandable response. Staying as composed and confident as a green-hued super-lawyer is hard to do, but follow Jennifer's lead: Even if smashing feels like the best solution, stay levelheaded. There are many avenues to solving conflict, and being a hero is about using all your physical *and* mental skills to find a solution.

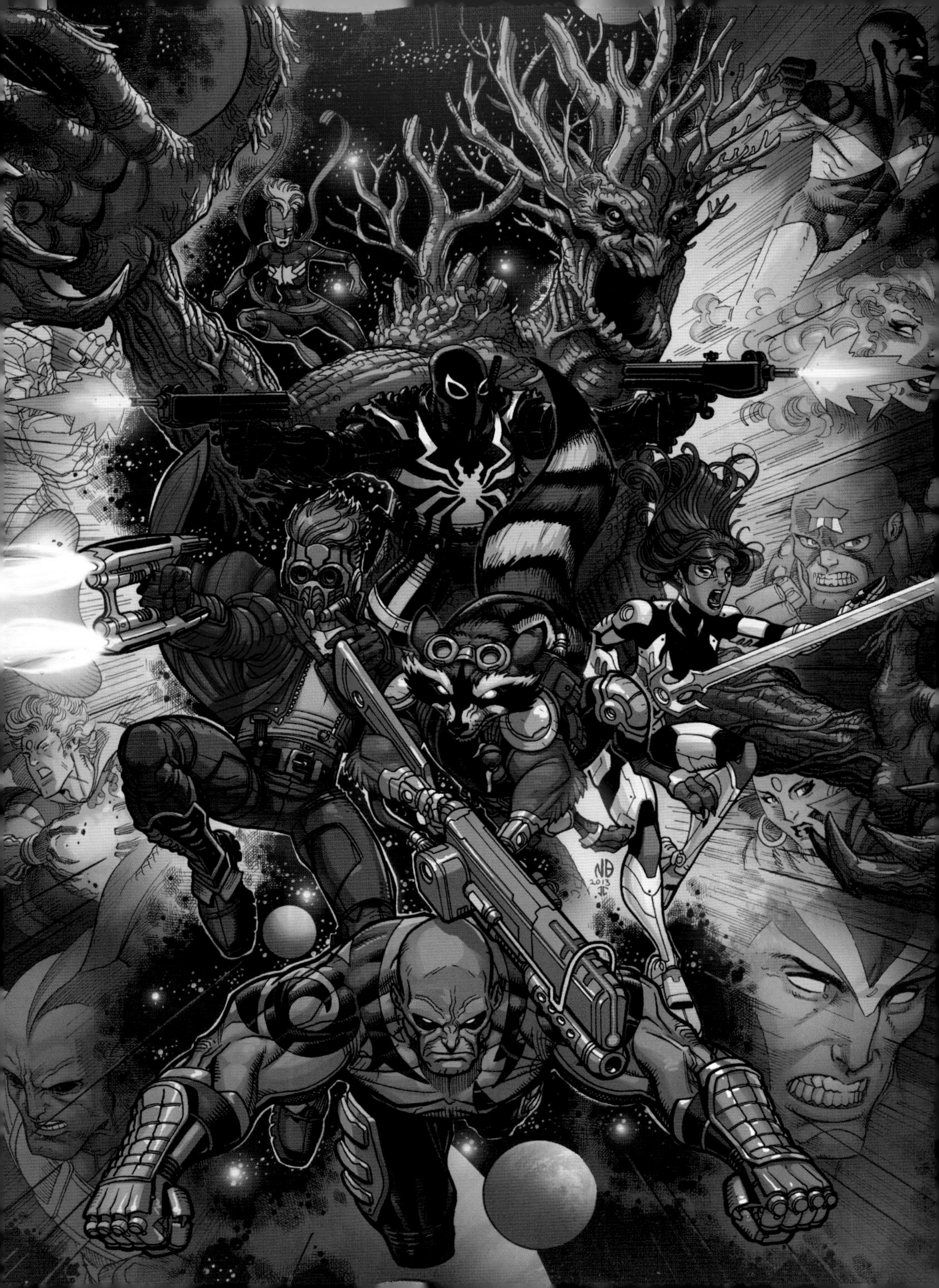
NB
2013

DEFY EXPECTATIONS

Nothing beats an underdog story. Formed by Peter Quill—Star-Lord himself—the Guardians of the Galaxy's first lineup consisted of Rocket Raccoon, Groot, Phyla-Vell, Gamora, Drax, Adam Warlock, Mantis, and a telepathic Russian dog named Cosmo. Not your typical heroes, this ragtag group of intergalactic outlaws are hardly your ideal saviors of the universe. Initially just thrown together, this group has chosen to remain a team, taking on threats with a headstrong manner and little to no plan. Yet somehow, it works.

Despite the Guardians' odd mix of personalities, they manage to pull together to defeat common enemies. And their villains aren't small-time; the big bads they fight are actually very big and very, very bad, from Thanos the Mad Titan to Ronan the Accuser, and even Emperor J'Son of Spartax, otherwise known as Peter Quill's biological father, who later took on the not-at-all sinister sounding moniker of Mister Knife. Against insurmountable foes, the Guardians give it their all and prove they've got what it takes.

If you're feeling undervalued or unappreciated, beware letting others' low expectations get into your head; sometimes the prediction can become a reality. Instead, hold strong. The Guardians don't let others' opinions define them; instead, they turn galaxies upside down. Channel that intergalactic bravado and do your best to do your best, and you can determine your own outcome. Defy expectations not to prove others wrong but to prove to yourself that anything is possible.

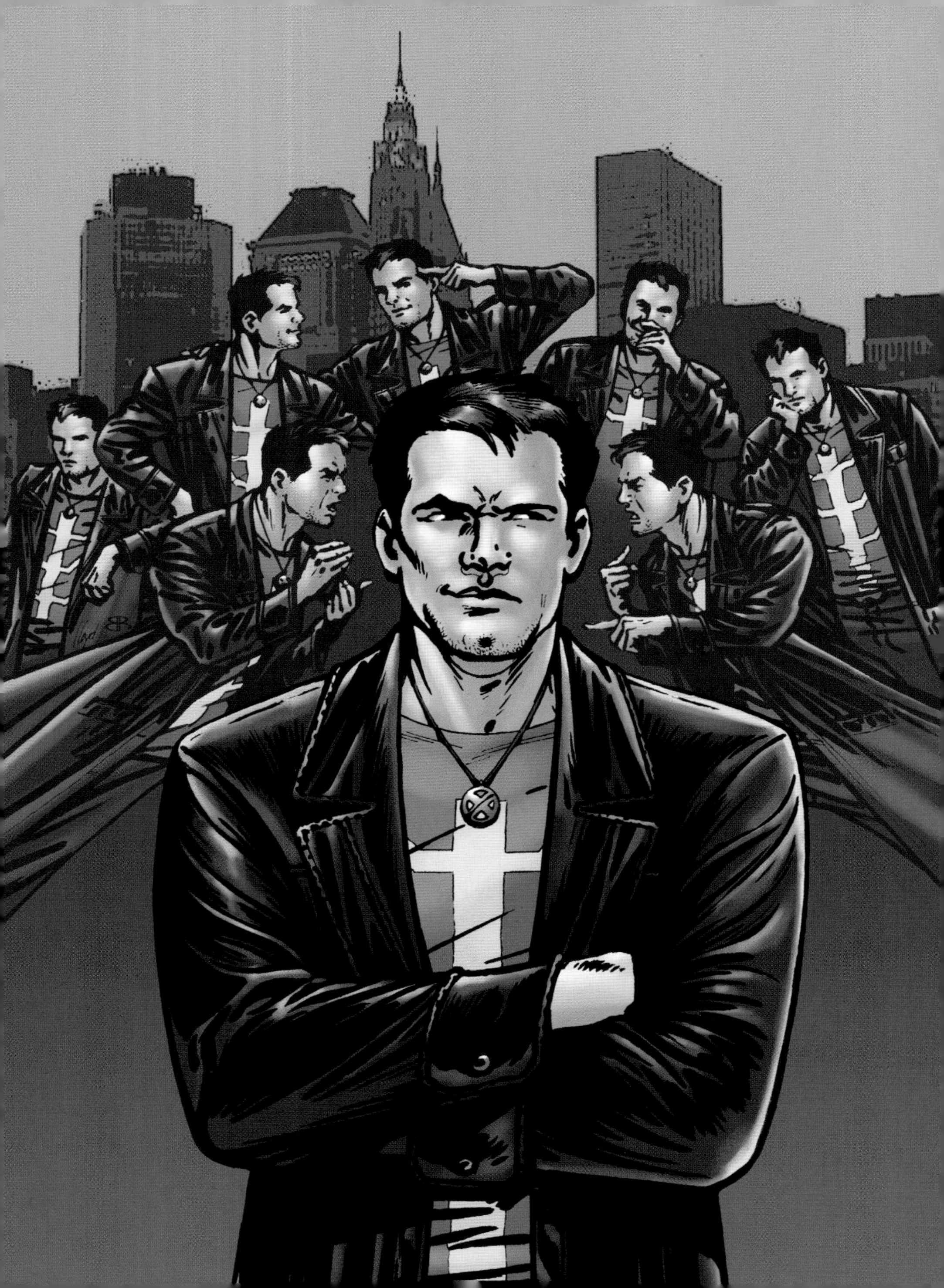

DON'T BE AFRAID TO SAY NO

Saying no on repeat is healthy, even if you live in a world where infinite duplicates of you exist. Jamie Madrox's life was forever changed when his mutant powers manifested and he began replicating. He tried wearing a suit to neutralize his powers, but nothing could stop the process. Even worse, when his duplicates were killed, Madrox experienced psychic backlash. For him, chasing after these multiples was an exhausting task that eventually took its toll.

Due to his unique powers, Jamie was often invited to join the X-Men and fight alongside other mutants. Time and again, he declined, choosing instead to live a simpler life. It wasn't that he shied away from a good fight; though he fought alongside others as a member of various teams, he always knew that following his own path was his end goal.

Life would be so much easier if we all had duplicates so we could try out every scenario that comes our way. When multitudinous offers appear but none quite fit into your life, it may be hard to say no. Could you be making the wrong choice? Possibly, but you need to go with your gut and do what's right for you. Are you backing down from a challenge? Backing down isn't defeat—it's like deciding to take a break on your own terms. Knowing when to decline an opportunity is a bold move—and a decision that will ultimately serve you over and over and over . . . and over again.

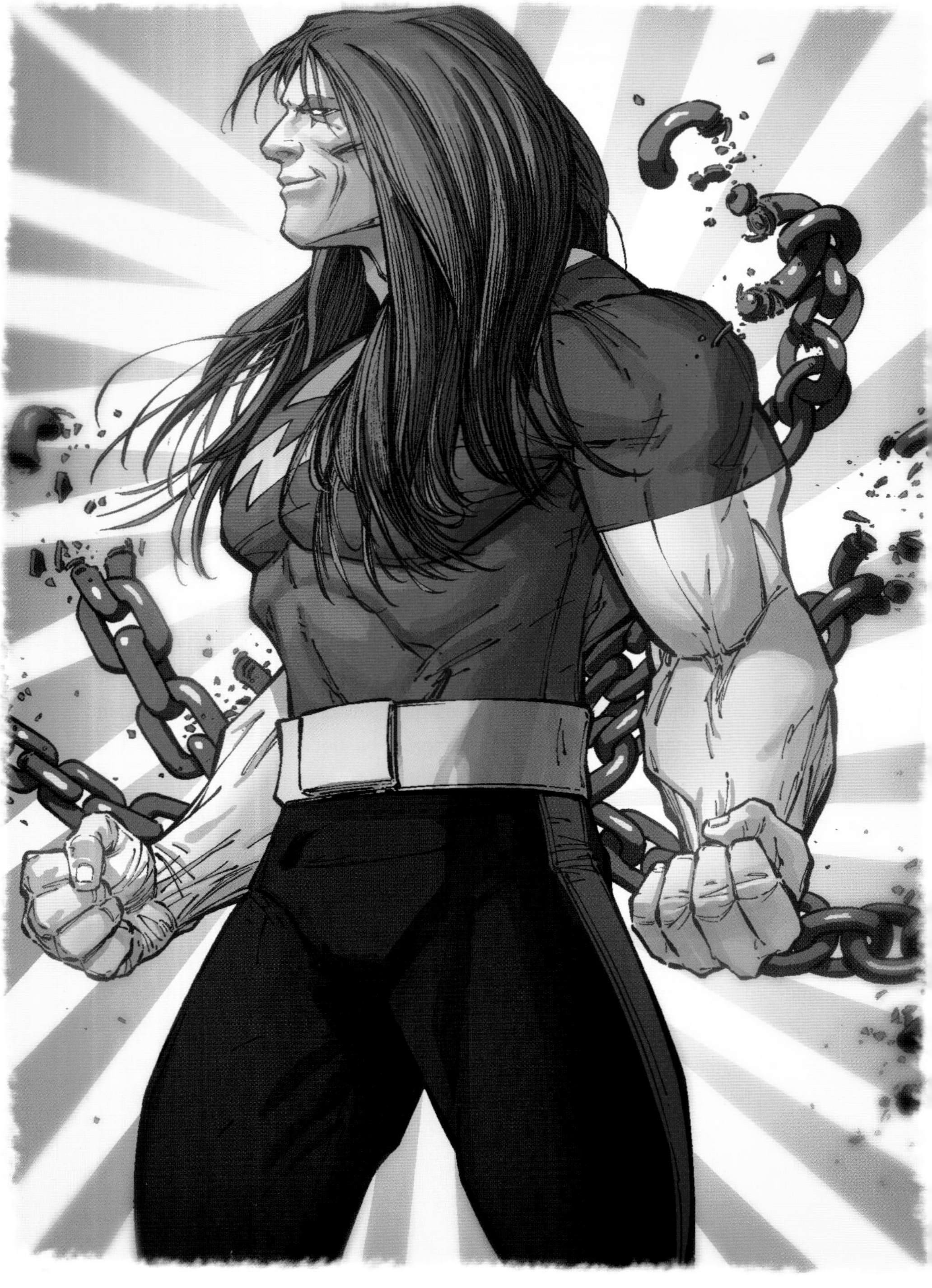

ASK FOR HELP

When super heroes need help, who do they turn to? Their own personal psychologist, that's who. Dr. Leonard Samson, "Doc" for short, is the go-to physician for heroes in need. A doctor of psychiatry, Samson was first hired by General Thaddeus "Thunderbolt" Ross to cure his daughter Betty after a blood transfusion with Sandman went wrong and gave her a crystalline form. Using some of the Hulk's gamma energy, Doc was able to cure both Betty's physical transformation and Hulk's unstable temperament. The process exposed Samson to gamma radiation, giving him superhuman strength. Balancing a professional life with enhanced powers then became a daily struggle for Doc.

Having to wrestle with his own personality's good and evil sides means this doctor understands the vulnerable positions in which his clients often find themselves. While the yin and yang of his own plight gives Doc dangerously intimate insights, his psychological prowess can't do it all. He knows he must turn to others for assistance, which pulls him—and his patients—through every time.

If psychiatrists with super powers need to ask for help once in a while, so can you. Asking for help is not a weakness. It takes strength to realize you can't go it alone. If you don't have any gamma radiation on hand, take the time to seek the aid of a professional. Acknowledging that you need a bit of extra help is a good way to nurture the best, healthiest version of you.

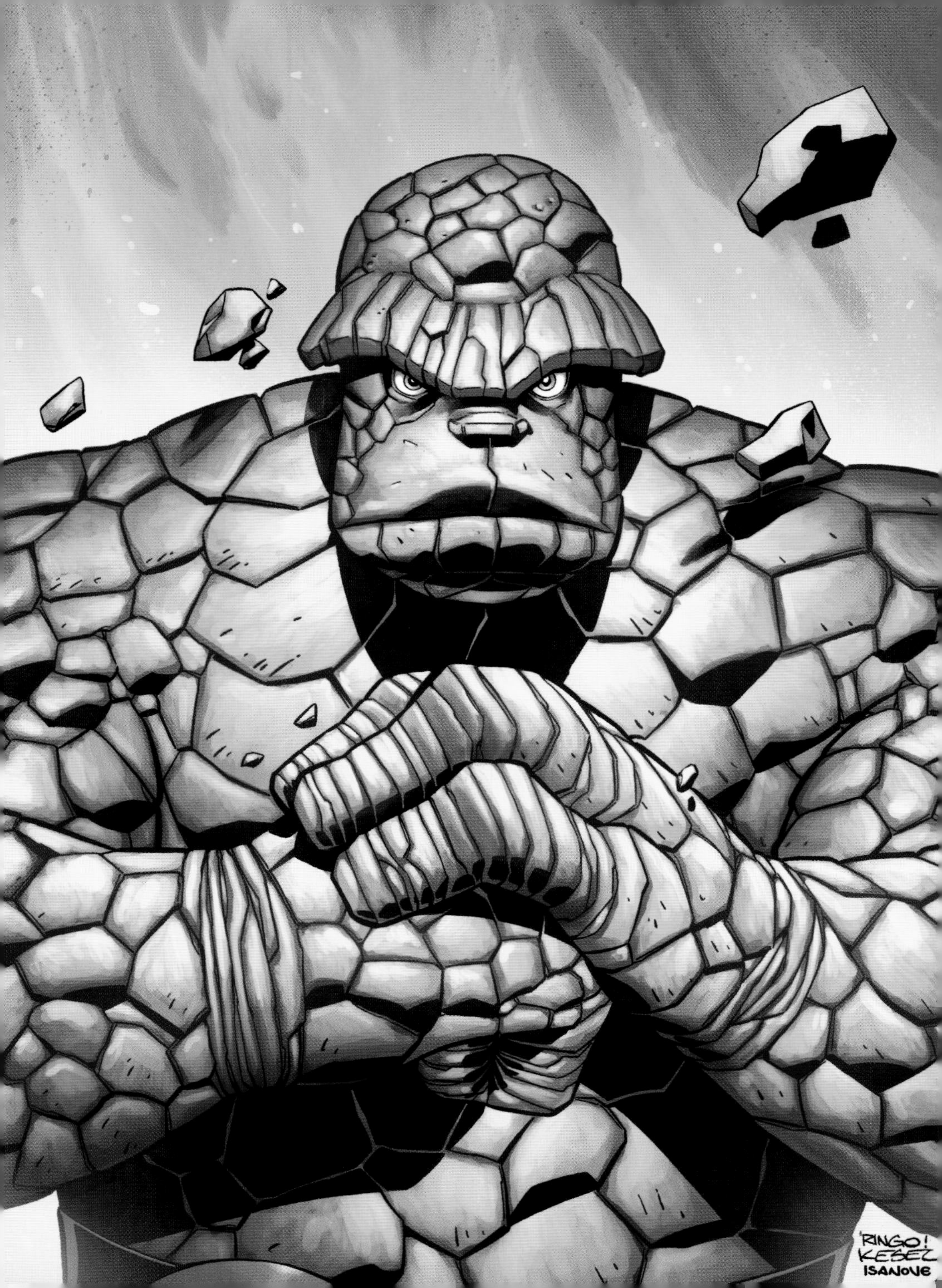
RINGO!
KESEL
ISANOVE

BE HUMBLE

Braggadocio and a boisterous personality seem to go hand in hand for some super heroes. But believe it or not, it is possible to save the world and not hold a press conference alerting everyone to your accomplishments. (We get it, Namor, you think you're superior.) We all should be proud of the things we've achieved, but knowing when to humble yourself is a power that's unmatched.

Ben Grimm's transformation into the Thing put him in the awkward position of people judging him on his physical appearance before getting to know him. His foreboding presence, coupled with his signature phrase, "It's clobberin' time!" is a little over the top, but Ben himself is anything but. Through it all he does his job without requiring much fanfare, proving that you don't need to be loud about your achievements when you believe in yourself and the work you're doing. (Plus, the Human Torch talks enough for everyone.) Ben's humble attitude toward life is what makes him a caring hero who underneath it all is still the same guy from Yancy Street.

Being understated can be mistaken for being shy, but keeping your achievements in check allows you to have a level head and excel even further in your endeavors. Knowing when to shout your wins from the rooftops and when to keep it on the low is a skill not everyone can manage elegantly. Let Ben be your guide: Stay true to yourself, work hard, accept both praise and criticism. Being humble will empower you to be even better.

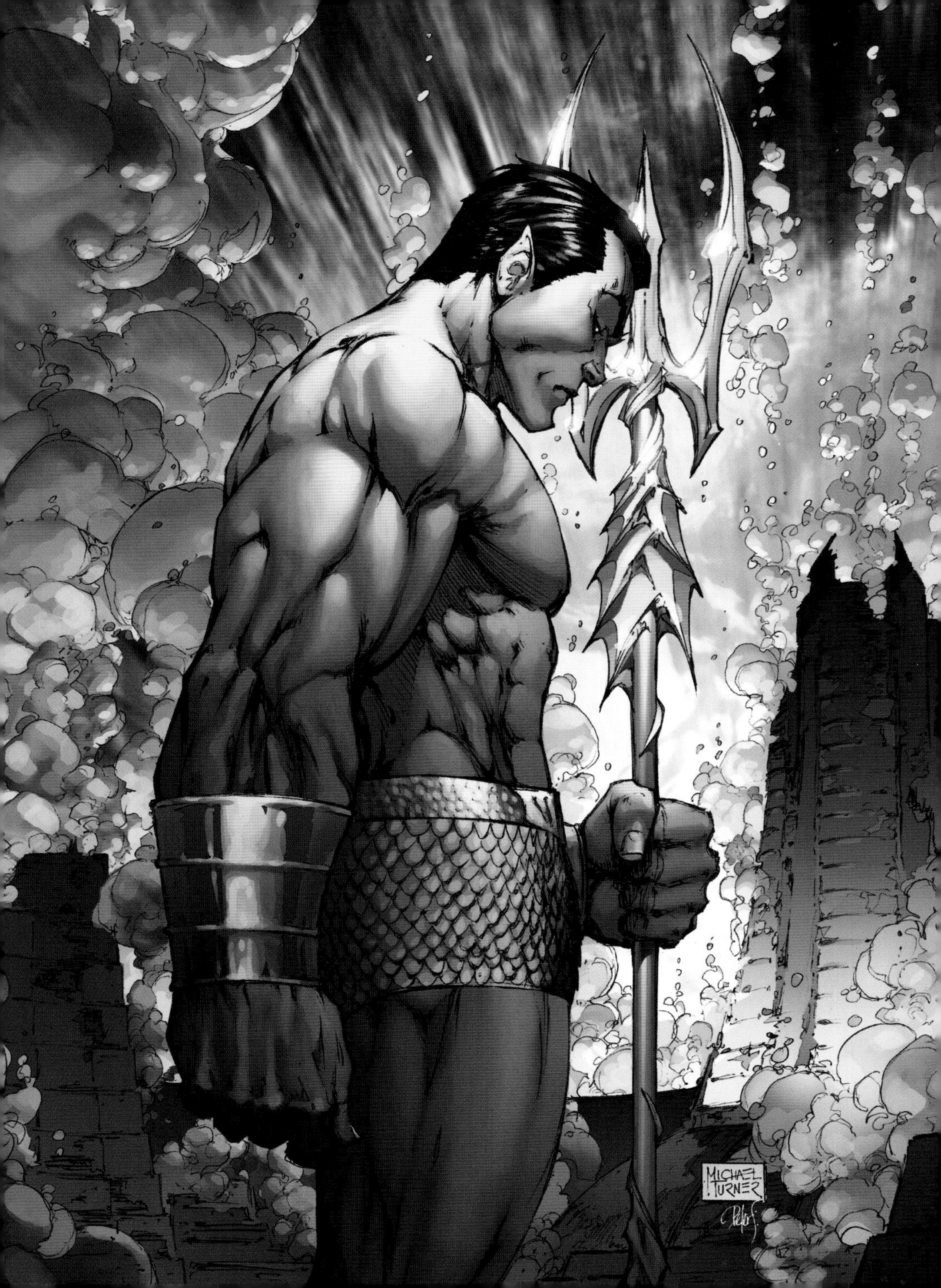
MICHAEL TURNER

STAND BY YOUR CONVICTIONS

Sticking to your beliefs can be seen as just being obstinate—and for Namor, ruler of Atlantis, sometimes that's not far off. (It's hard to water down your ego when you rule the entirety of the sea.) When it comes to supporting and protecting his people, Namor will never back down. Atlantis comes first, and any threat toward the Atlantean way of life, he takes personally.

When Tony Stark invited Namor, Reed Richards, Professor Xavier, Black Bolt, and Doctor Strange into his secret society, the Illuminati, Namor had his doubts about joining. He finally broke with the group when Tony decided to shoot Hulk into space to protect the world. Seeing a friend turn on a friend went against everything the noble royal stood for. He stood up for what he believed was right, and he walked away from the Illuminati to protect his people in his own way.

Like the dark depths of Atlantis, deciding whether to go along with a group or stick to your own principles can sometimes feel murky. Namor uses his catchphrase, "Imperius Rex!" as a rallying cry; likewise, find your own (perhaps less verbal) motivation that will let your convictions be the luminous light that will always guide you home. The decision you stand by will inevitably strengthen your belief in yourself—and others' faith in you as well.

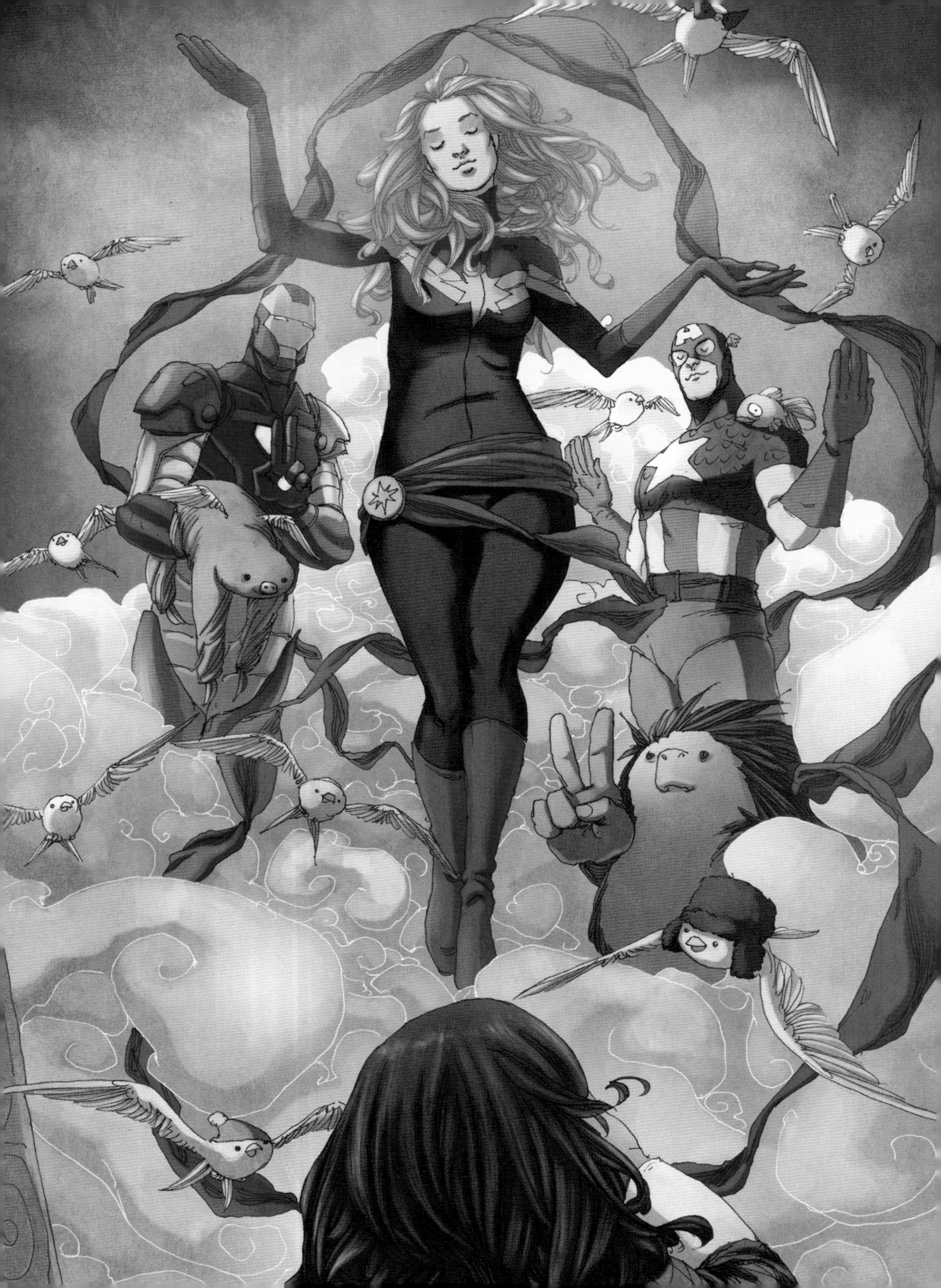

UNLOCK YOUR POTENTIAL

Harness the possibilities within yourself, and you just might be surprised. Originally created as a result of a Kree science experiment, the Inhumans have their powers unlocked when they contact Terrigen Mist. When young Inhumans come of age, Terrigenesis is a rite of passage. Not all Inhumans have genes fit for adapting to this process, but for others, the exposure to Terrigen Mist can trigger a transformation that taps into their hidden potential.

When the Terrigen Mists are released across the globe, people who unknowingly have Inhuman genes begin to transform into their Inhuman form. This unexpectedly allows them to harness their inherent powers and develop once-hidden abilities. These new powers are overwhelming for some, but for others they open a whole new world that has been buried inside them.

Most of us may not have hidden super-human genes, but we all have something inside of us waiting to be released. Be it an artistic talent, a thirst for knowledge, or even resilience in emotional situations, we may not even know this potential exists. You don't need to save the world, but when you look deeper into yourself, you may find something that you didn't know you had. Have you always felt like you wanted to write a book? Had an inkling to sing in public? Lean into these talents, channel them with gusto, and you may find a whole other side of yourself waiting to emerge.

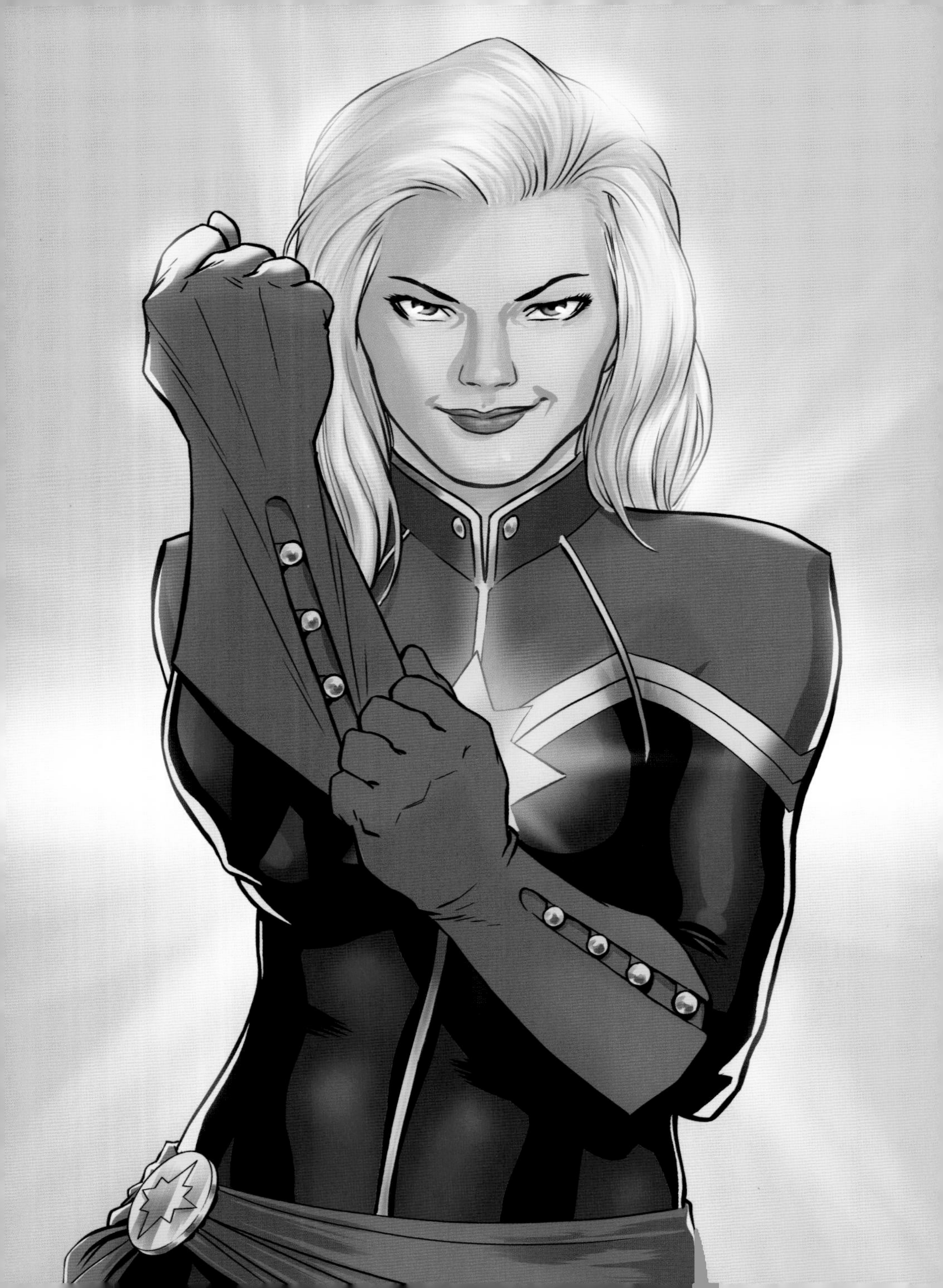

WHEN YOU'RE KNOCKED DOWN, GET BACK UP AGAIN

Often underestimated, never undeterred, Carol Danvers has always defied the odds. She dreams of going to space and, despite an abusive father, joins the United States Air Force, rises in the ranks, and attains her dream by joining NASA. There she meets Dr. Walter Lawson, who is secretly the Kree spy Mar-Vell. Mar-Vell fights his rival, Yon-Rogg, resulting in the altering of Carol's DNA, making her half-Kree and giving her super-powers. In another setback, Carol is attacked by Rogue—then a member of the Brotherhood of Evil Mutants—who absorbs Carol's powers and core memories, leaving her in a coma. Later, Carol suffers brain damage so traumatic that she loses all her memories.

She co-founds the first team of all-female Avengers, A-Force. And her legendary heroics also inspire a young heroine named Kamala Khan. No matter what life serves her, Carol always bounces back. It's this determination that makes her a trustworthy team member and exemplary leader as Captain Marvel.

How you deal with failure is a testament to your own fortitude. Nevertheless, responding to a dismal situation can instill long-lasting trauma, and moving on can be difficult. Focus on reprioritizing your purpose and find new ways to heal in order to forge ahead: keep yourself active, meet with friends, enjoy your favorite hobbies, do whatever you can to lift your spirits. And like the illustrious Captain herself, you will fly higher than ever.

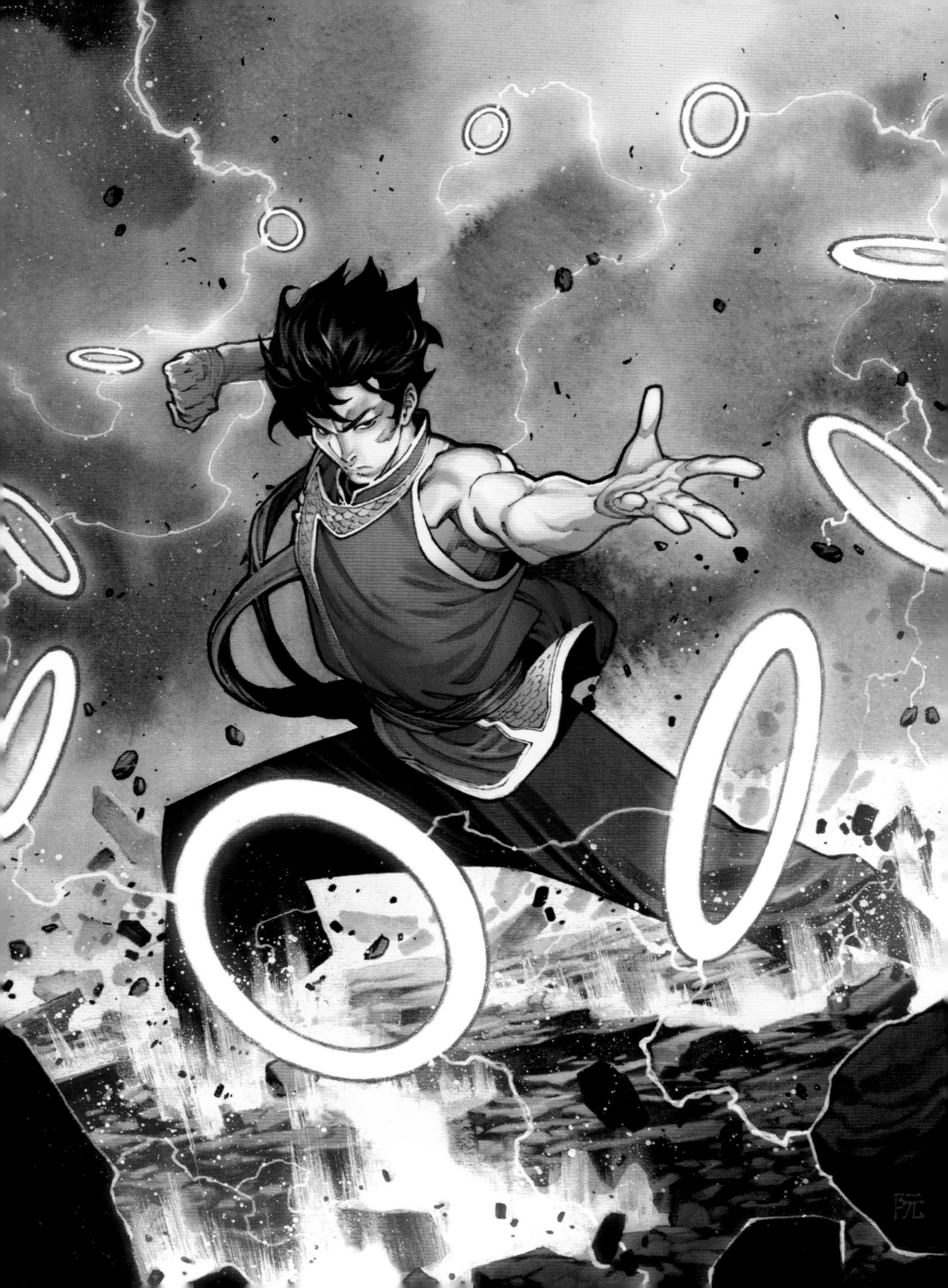

YOU DETERMINE YOUR OWN FUTURE

Grab the rings and take control of your own destiny. It's hard to focus on your future when your father is as villainous as they come. From raising other children as "sons" to battle Shang-Chi, to resurrecting lost ancestors and even trying to knock the moon out of orbit—when your own parent has that much hostility, it's hard not to find and take the low road. However, Shang-Chi uses meditation and his chi, or internal energy, to find focus, perseverance, and calm, controlling his emotions and forging his own path.

Shang-Chi has been trained as a living weapon, skilled in martial arts and philosophical disciplines. Then his familial loyalty becomes sullied when he finds out about his father's nefarious dealings. Using his physical and mental prowess, he vows to fight for justice, and although this makes him the enemy—and a target—of his very own father, he lets nothing deter him from his mission.

Like Shang-Chi, you can take what you've learned from your past and decide your own future. Whether it's the weight of family obligations or simple loyalty, letting go of something that is a huge part of you physically, culturally, and psychologically can be difficult—but it's always important. You can choose your own destiny—even if your parent isn't a member of a sinister secret society.

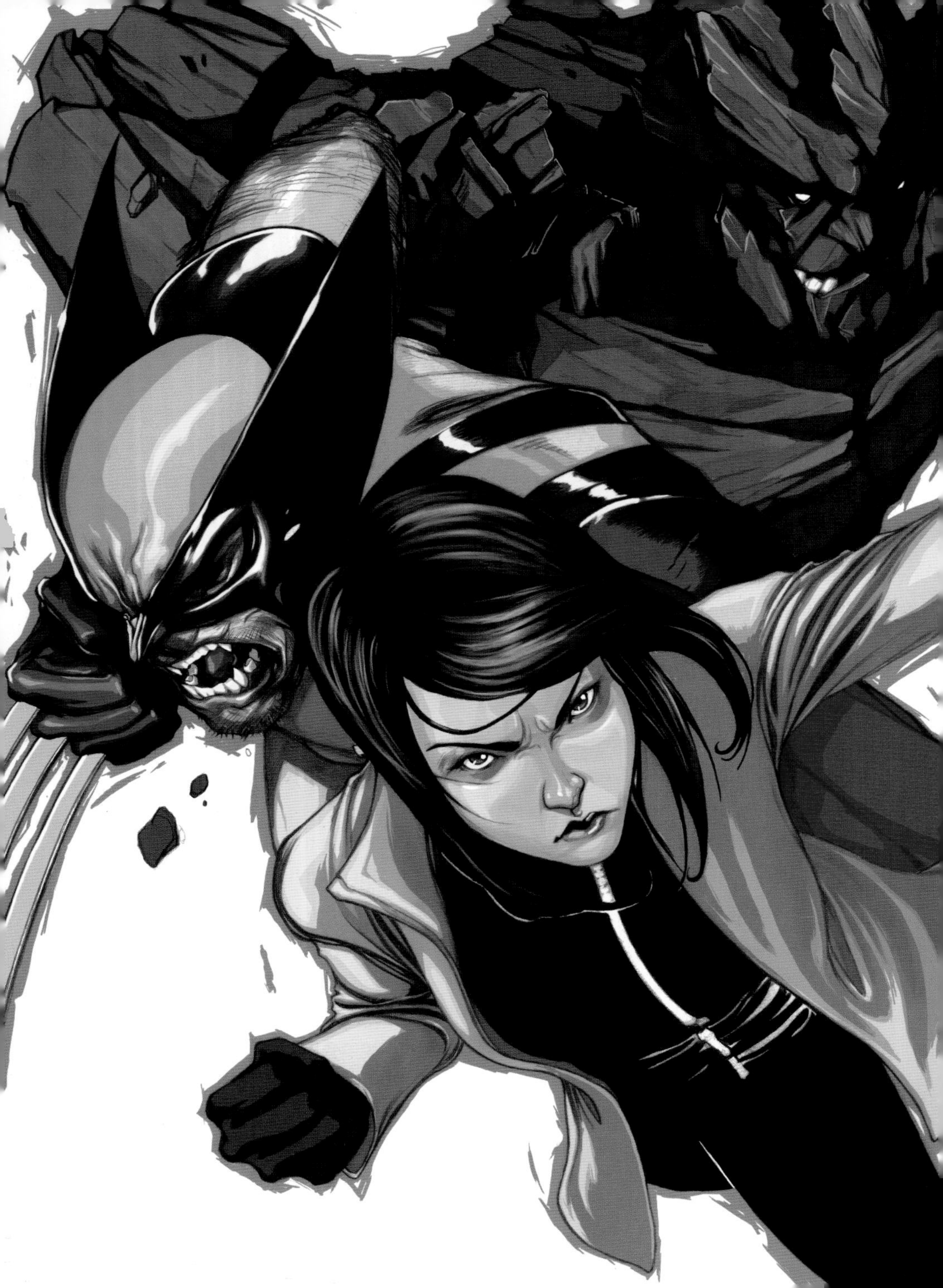

AGE DOESN'T DEFINE ACHIEVEMENTS

It's easy to dismiss youth for inexperience or old age for weakness. During Jubilation Lee's early days with the X-Men, she is often underestimated as their youngest member. An orphan who found refuge in the most teen place of all, the mall, Jubilee has an energy and innocence that give her an edge whether she's in a fight or working with a team.

Elder statesmen can sometimes feel out of touch, but when needed, their advice and experience is invaluable. Jubilee has looked to many mentors, from Wolverine and Banshee to Emma Frost, for guidance. These storied X-Men give her the direction she needs to come into her own and learn how to lead—and to be led. Like most kids trying to find themselves, Jubilee is often discounted due to her adolescence, yet she eventually grows into a confident leader and team member, all while keeping her youthful energy.

Whatever your age, don't let that number determine what you can and can't do. Use your youthfulness—or your seasoned maturity—to your advantage. Listen to your mentors and use their advice to forge your own path. Whether you're sixteen or sixty, there is so much more to accomplish, so rev up your pyrotechnic plasmoids, take advantage of your spirited energy, and show 'em what you got.

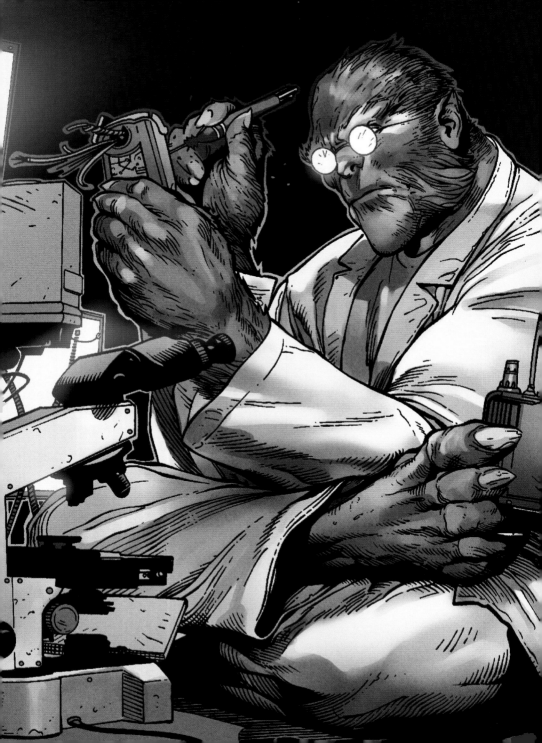

IT'S WHAT'S ON THE INSIDE THAT COUNTS

Don't judge a book by its cover, especially when that cover is a hairy blue brute. Henry "Hank" McCoy was born a mutant due to his father's exposure to massive amounts of radiation. His strength and athletic abilities are second only to his intellectual prowess. While at Xavier's School for Gifted Youngsters, Hank takes a hormonal extract that causes genetic mutation and quickly grows fur and fangs, changing him into an actual Beast. He soon realizes that most people will never see past his monstrous countenance.

As a genius, Hank learns to combine his intellect with his beast-like appearance. An indispensable member of the X-Men, Hank continues his genetic research and studies, using his superior intelligence to help people overcome the prejudice that his outward appearance elicits—showing not only that human–mutant interactions can be safe but also that personality rules over physical appearance.

Before you judge someone, be they mutant or human, look beyond what's presented to you. Getting to know someone's true character takes time and effort, but the investment is worth it. Take time to look deeper and keep an open mind. So if you see a blue-haired beast hanging upside down in the Danger Room, don't judge. Even the most intelligent beings are allowed their proclivities.

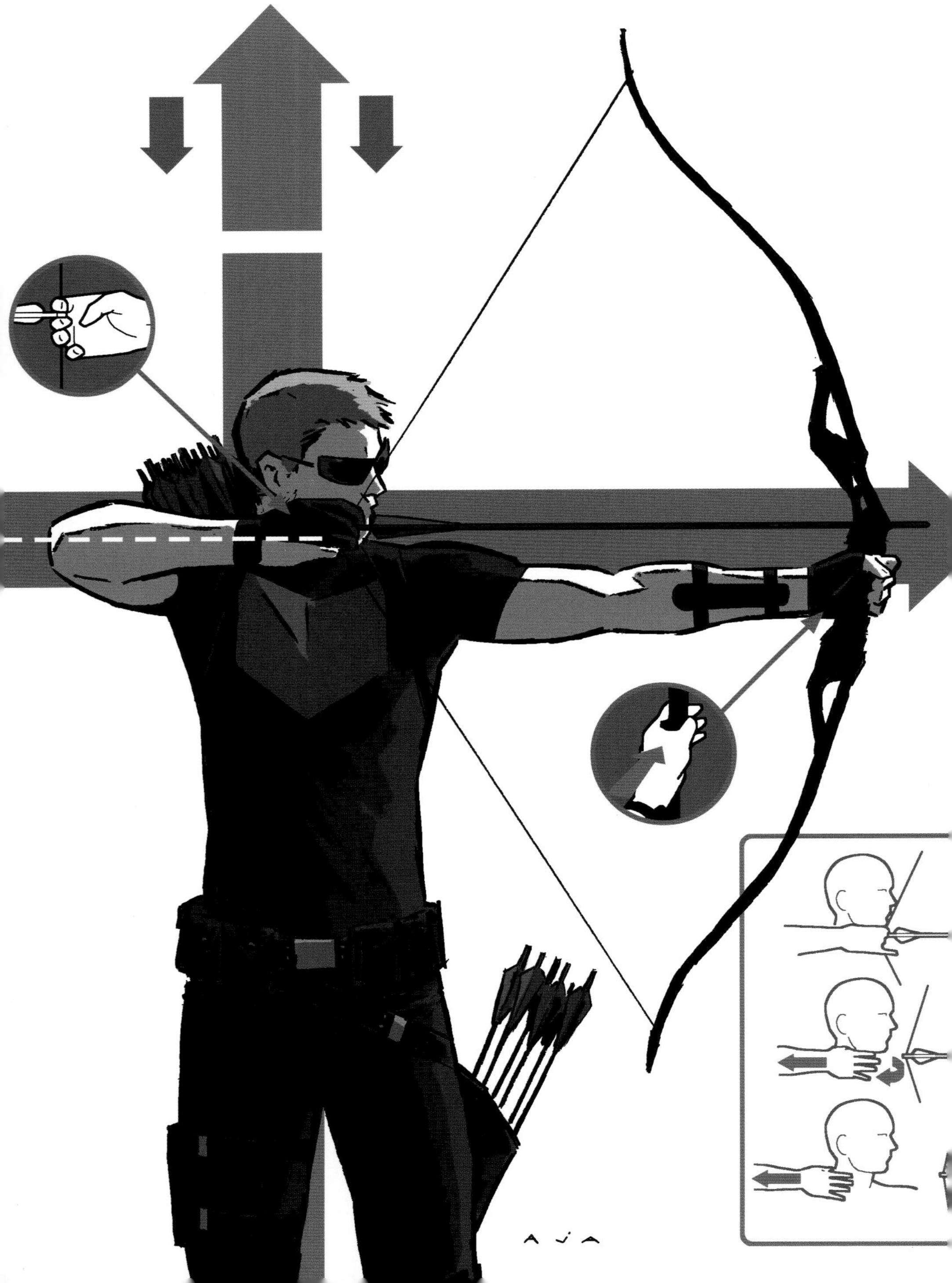
AJA

STAY FOCUSED

Set your sights on the bull's-eye. Clint Barton may be a hero without any super powers, but what he does have is tenacity and perseverance. Also known as Hawkeye, he was orphaned at a young age and practiced and perfected his archery skills under pressure. He has trick arrows up his sleeve, but it's his marksmanship that sets him apart. Hawkeye's hyper-specialized abilities require unwavering precision, a focus that sets him apart from the rest.

Before his crimefighting career, Clint actually debuts as a villain, clashing with Iron Man, but this one-time outlaw turns his life around. Super-powerless, Clint uses determination not only to fight alongside super heroes but also to lead them. That he could step up to this task is incredibly meaningful given his beginnings and shows that his attentiveness and attitude are acknowledged and rewarded.

Staying the course to realize your dreams takes energy, determination, and willpower. Whether your goals are financial, physical, or work–life balance, concentrate on your objective. Nock your arrow in your bow. Channel your energy and follow through. Your focus will lead you to your target.

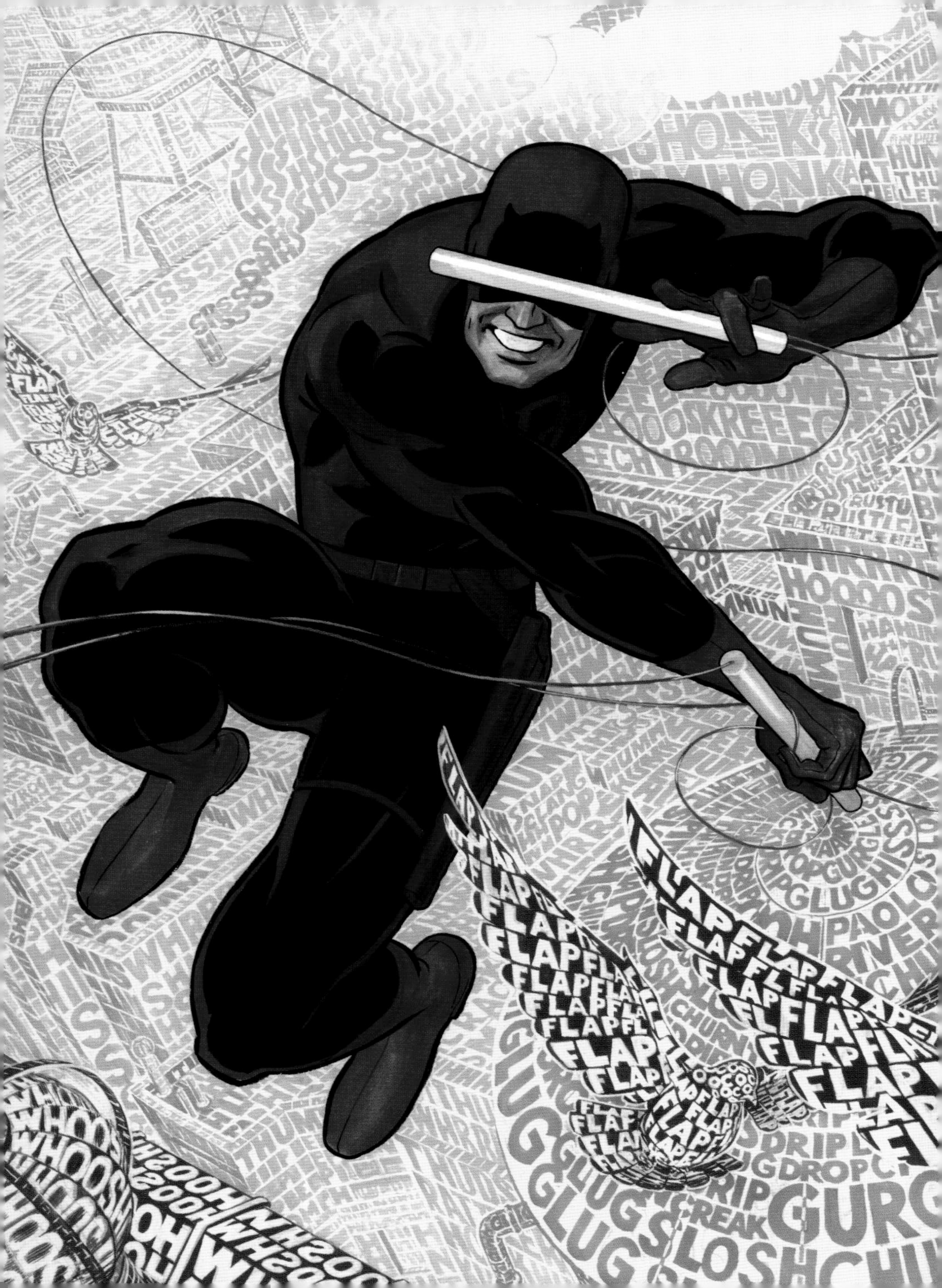
FLAP
WHOOSH
GLUG
SLOSH
DRIP
CREAK
GURG
HONK
CHURN
POP

TRUST YOUR INSTINCTS

Imagine if your obstacles only enhanced your abilities. Blinded by radioactive waste as a child, which also heightened his other senses and gave him a new "radar" sense, Matt Murdock fights crime as a lawyer during the day and physically battles the underworld by night as the masked vigilante hero Daredevil.

The tragic death of his father pushed Matt into law. In the courtroom and on the streets, he depends on his instincts to bring criminals to justice. When facing the infamous Kingpin, Matt's strength and fighting prowess intimidate his enemy, and it's his understanding of his nemesis's mind that allows him to dig even deeper into the criminal psyche. His instincts are his secret weapon.

That "gut feeling" you have? That's real. It's your mind and body working together to alert you of oncoming happiness or straight-up impending doom. But actually trusting your instincts . . . now that's a whole other level of understanding. Matt quickly had to learn to follow his gut feelings. With no radar sense, you may need a little more time to get in tune with yours, but once you get a handle on them, you'll feel more self-assured and resolute in your actions.

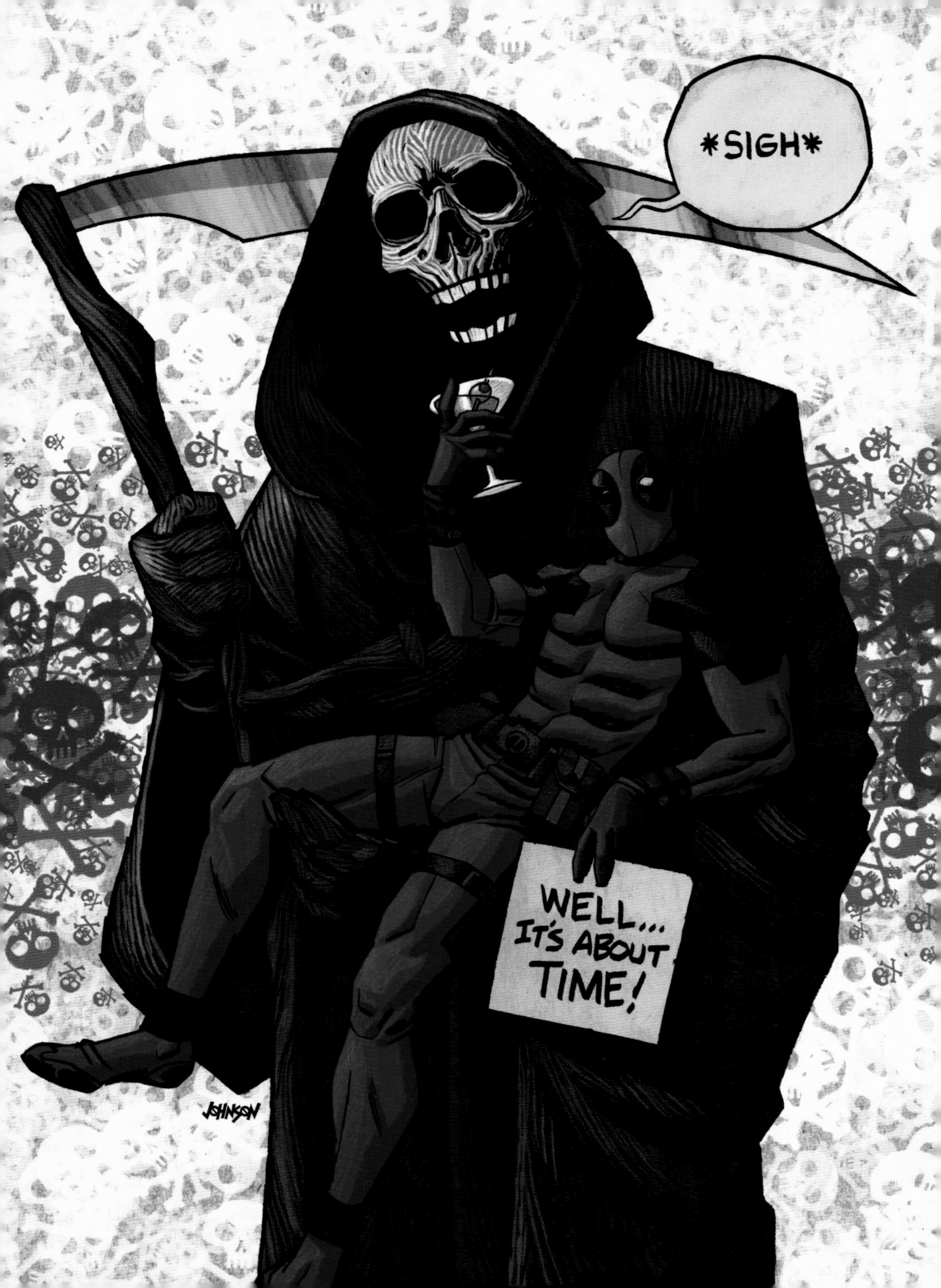
SIGH
WELL... IT'S ABOUT TIME!
JOHNSON

DON'T TAKE YOURSELF TOO SERIOUSLY

Joke's on you, literally. If there were a living embodiment of the phrase, "Don't take yourself too seriously," it would be Deadpool. An assassin who received a healing factor thanks to the Weapon X program, Wade Wilson is a self-made man, in the sense that he can recover and generate body parts. (Get it?) His wise-cracking, almost offensive demeanor earned him the nickname "the Merc with the Mouth," and does he ever earn it. He rarely stops talking, which is part of his powers: his nonstop chatter disarms and confuses his enemies.

You never know what you're going to get with Deadpool. A natural-born solo act, he once led a team of 'Pools that included Lady Deadpool, Kidpool, Dogpool, and even a zombified head known as Headpool. In keeping with the humorous hero's nature, they traveled in a ship called the *Bea Arthur*. He even once hung out with the ghost of Benjamin Franklin. (Don't ask.) The point is, Deadpool knows his wit is his weapon and he uses it to his advantage, keeping his enemies on their toes.

Knowing when to be whimsical and when to be serious is important. Yet, keeping things light can help you feel better mentally and physically and get you through the toughest of adventures. There's no better jolt of energy than a good laugh. Add that to the list of things that make you feel good—like chimichangas.

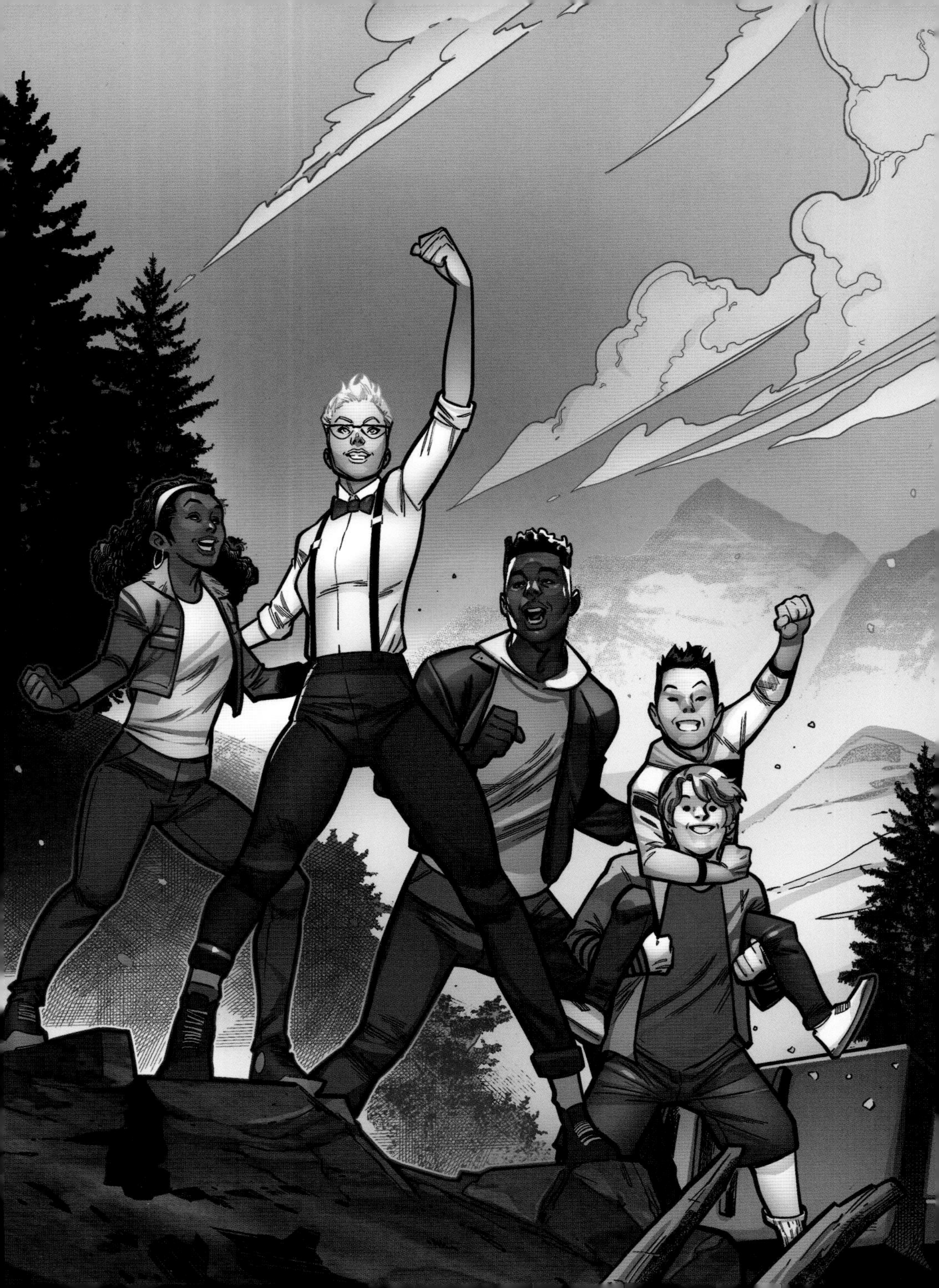

FIND YOUR PEOPLE

"Family is who you choose." And Benny Thomas, A.K.A. Marvel Guy should know as a member of the crimefighting Children of the Atom. Inspired by their favorite X-Men, Cherub (Gabe Brathwaite), Cyclops-Lass (Buddy Bartholomew), Gimmick (Carmen Maria Cruz), and brothers Marvel Guy (Benny Thomas) and Daycrawler (Jay Thomas, or as he prefers, Nighty Night Crawler) are a group of friends obsessed with mutants. These youthful X-Men sidekicks have a lot on their plate; while all are trying to find their place in the world, more often than not they're bogged down in their own inner turmoil.

It turns out that these heroes are regular non-mutant humans, but what makes them unique is their bond as marginalized teens struggling with their own issues. The group nearly breaks up when Carmen discovers that she actually has mutant powers; she is torn between two worlds, concerned about how her friends will view and accept her. Buddy's jealousy surfaces due to her devotion to mutantkind and her desire to have those powers herself, but in the end, she understands how special Carmen's gifts are, and their friendship and love help keep the team together.

Whether you have the most accepting family or you are on your own, surround yourself with people who love you no matter what, people who cheer you on during your highest of highs and are there to cradle you during your lowest lows. After all, even teen vigilantes like the Children of the Atom know that your crew is your everything.

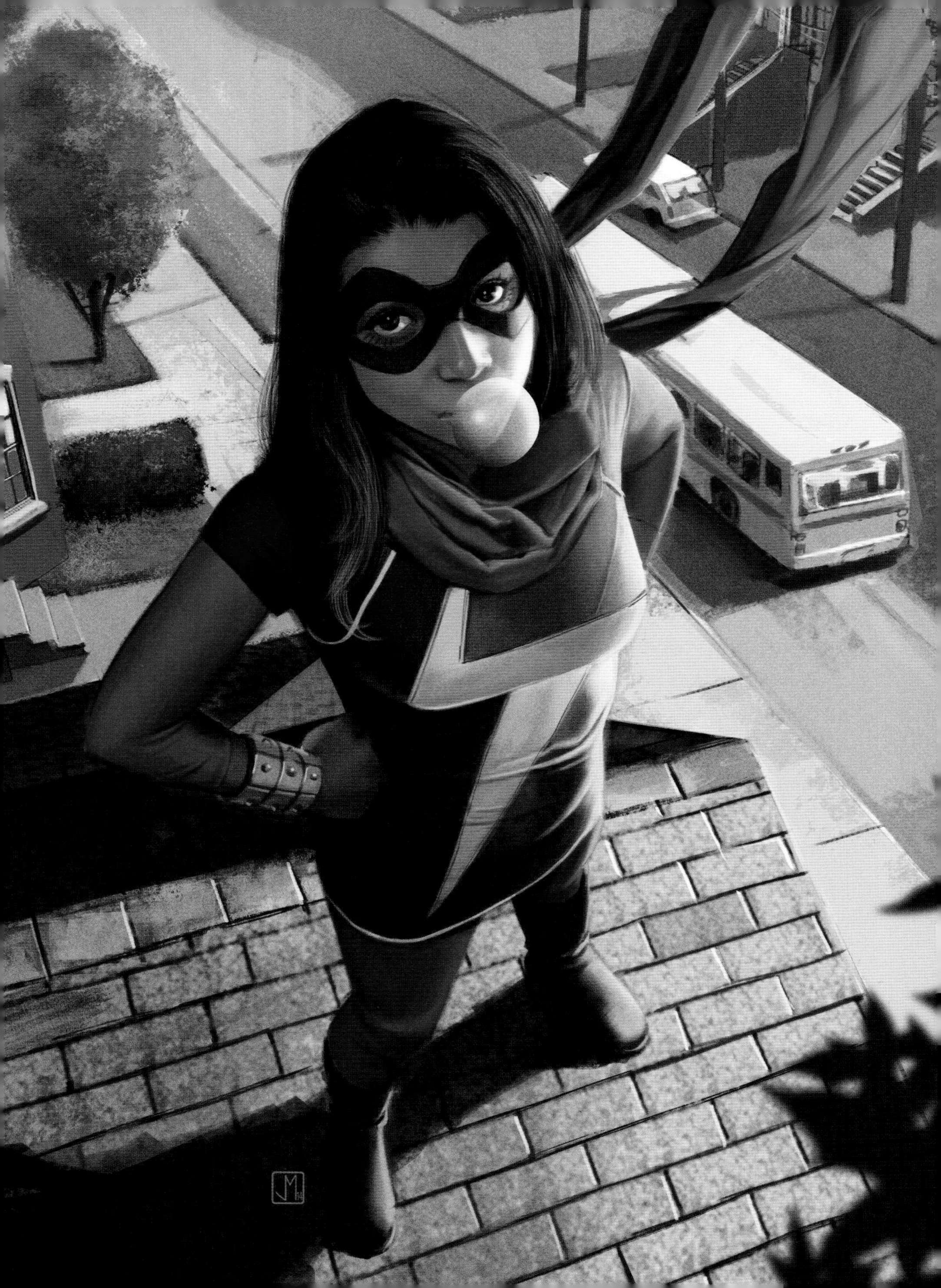

LEAN INTO YOUR IDENTITY

What's scarier—fighting a super villain or missing your strict parents' curfew? For Pakistani American Kamala Khan, it's about equal. Kamala is your normal, everyday young girl who idolizes her favorite heroes and does her best to fit in at school, all while wrestling with societal and cultural pressures. She's pretty average for a kid except for the fact that she also has Inhuman abilities.

Taking on the moniker of Ms. Marvel (the former name of her personal hero, Captain Marvel), Kamala has a level head and powers that allow her to extend her limbs and shift shape to fight crime. This Muslim American youth is as grounded as a girl carrying the weight of powers can be. She's a young person of color who fights crime, always keeping her community at front of mind. Her culture shapes her identity, with her supportive family encouraging and guiding her to stay true to her roots.

Growing up, we try out different personas before we discover our own identities, and sometimes our roads lead back to family and culture. Like Kamala, your identity might be shaped by your upbringing and surroundings. To find out, first you might need a little distance to embiggen yourself, to look at the values and principles of your heritage anew. Then, when you embrace your roots, you can allow them to guide your future.

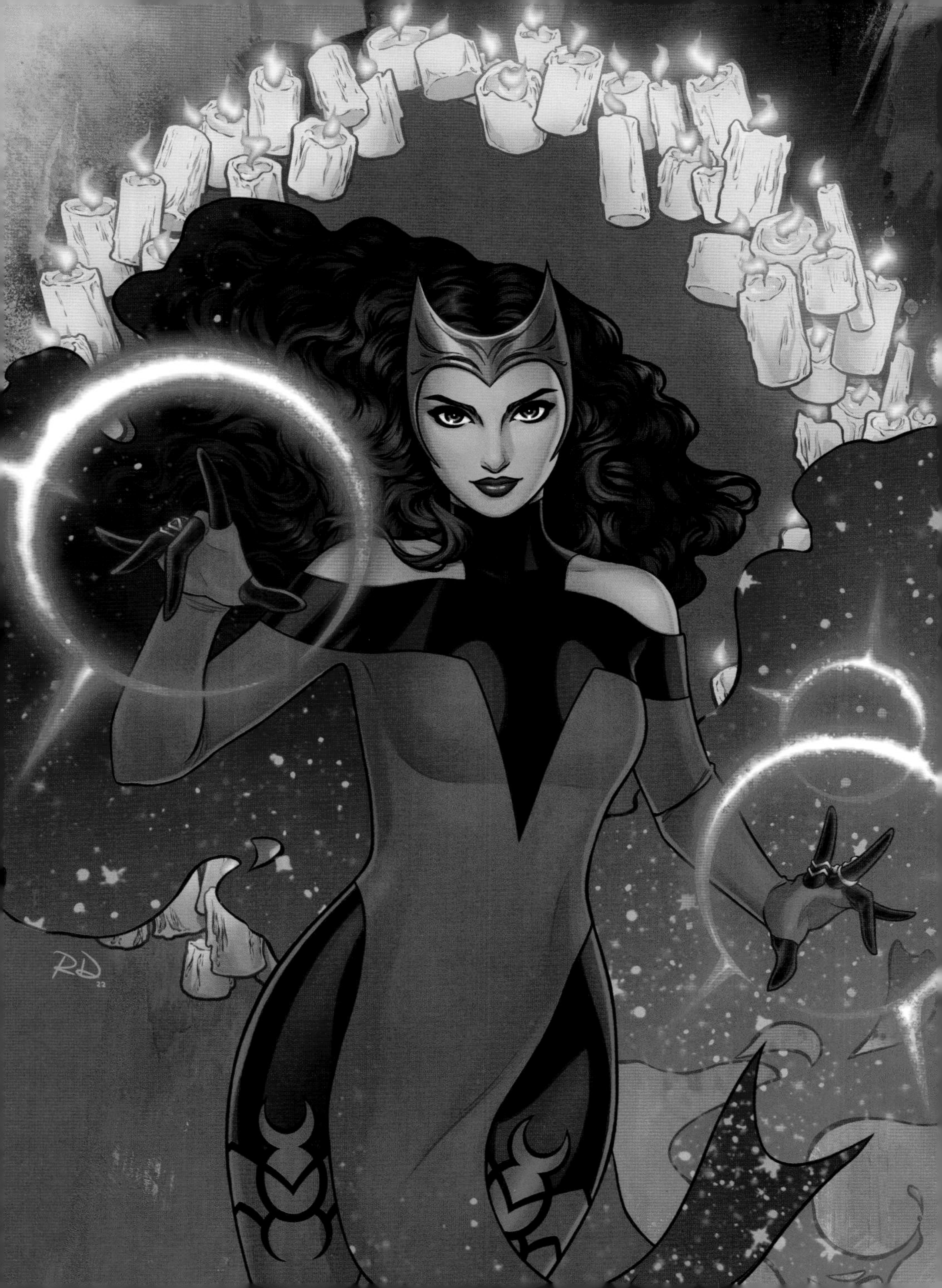

LET YOURSELF GRIEVE

The greatest power is allowing yourself to grieve. As a cautionary tale, take Wanda Maximoff—the Scarlet Witch—who may be one of the most powerful heroes of all, as her hexes give her the ability to manipulate reality. Yet as strong as she is, she has trouble letting go of her pain.

The death of a child would bring any parent to their knees. In the case of Wanda, it was losing her children that first prompts her psychological breakdown; when further threatened, she manipulates reality to create a world where mutants are superior, and she gets her "happily ever after." But things are not as they seem, and the eventual destruction of this world has great, damning consequences.

When you face trauma, there is no one way to deal with its effects, but hiding or holding on to stress can be damaging. Find a way to free yourself from it, such as speaking openly about it or engaging in physical activity. Let yourself go through the healing process, which can sometimes be painful, more painful than the cause of trauma itself. Wanda held on to her pain, and this led to wider destruction. Dealing with your grief in a safe and healthy way may better allow you to cope and, in time, recover.

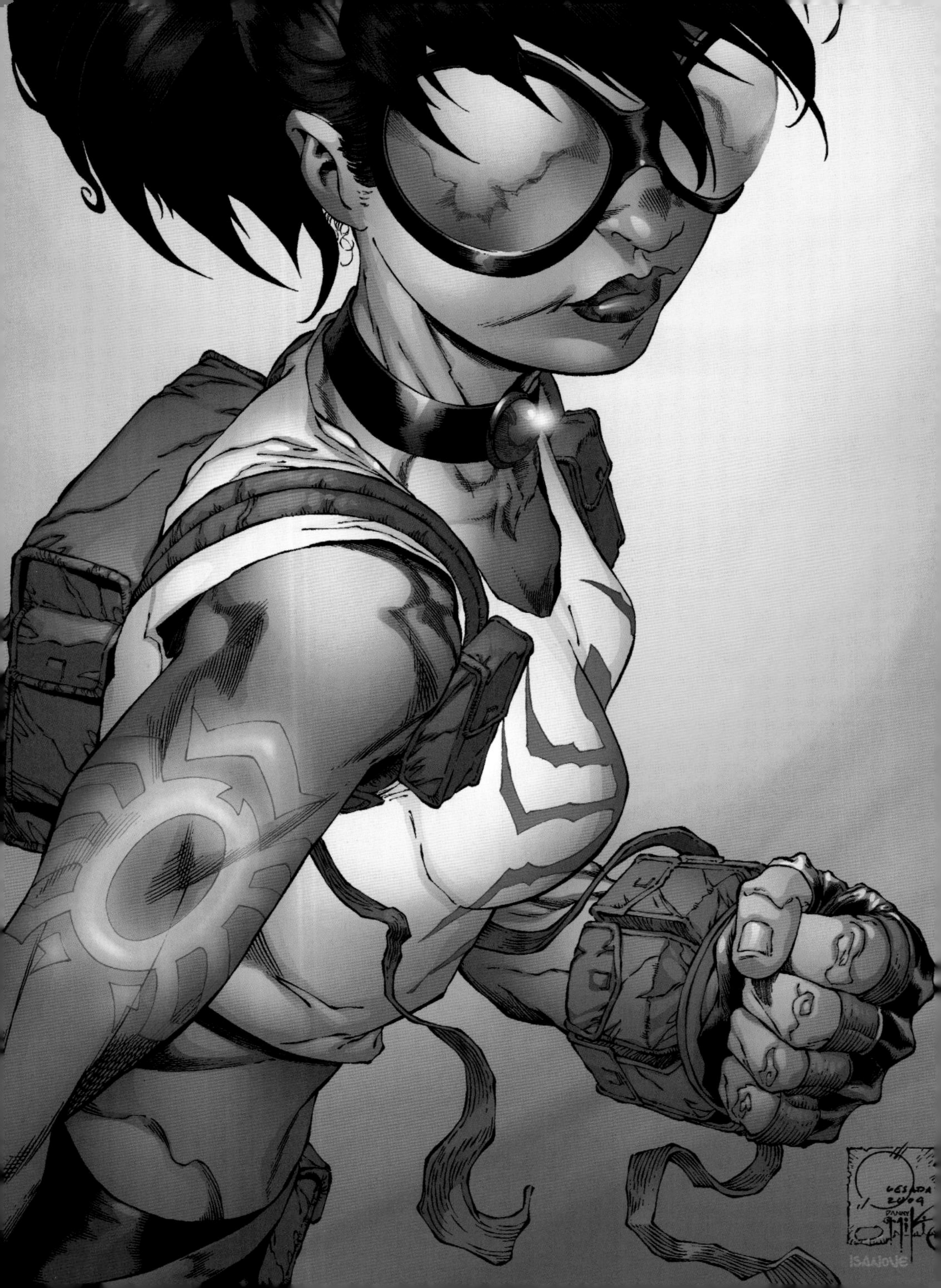

EMBRACE YOUR INDIVIDUALITY

Groups are great, but eventually you'll need to web-crawl out on your own. Like Aña "Anya" Corazón, anything but your normal teenage girl. She stumbles upon her powers by chance, finding herself in the middle of a battle between the Spider-Society and the Sisterhood of the Wasp. During the fight, the Spider-Society's Hunter is killed and the Mage, Miguel Legar, is supposed to bond with a new Hunter. Instead he bonds with Anya, triggering her dormant powers to engage a carapace armor that grows out of her tattoo, and she becomes Araña—the Spider.

Possessing superhuman strength and unique armor, Araña jumps right into the ancient order of the Spider-Society, whose fights against the Sisterhood lead her to work alongside the one and only Peter Parker in a battle that unfortunately results in Miguel's death. With Miguel gone, Araña leaves the Spider-Society, the only team she's known. Given the name of Spider-Girl by Spider-Woman, Araña finds purpose as her own hero, joining other teams like the Web Warriors and even the Avengers, yet always embracing her individuality while fighting evil.

As children, we're asked, "What do you want to be when you grow up?" The answers can vary from the determined to the irreverent, but the truth is this: We are always evolving. Like Anya, even if you change groups or teams, being able to showcase your special talents and embrace what makes you unique will help you stand out. Stand up and take a chance on your own terms, in a way that makes you happy and lets you be yourself.

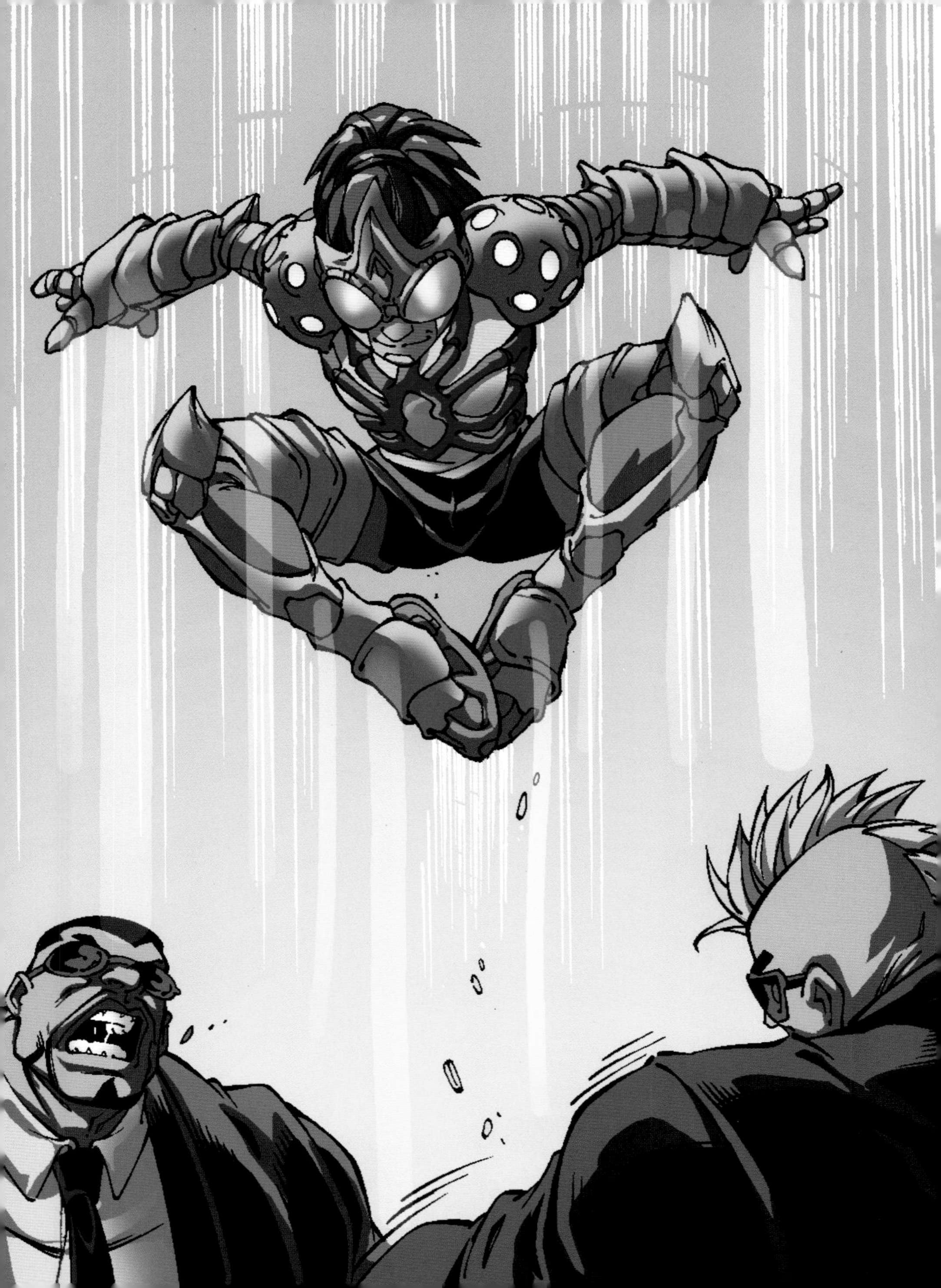

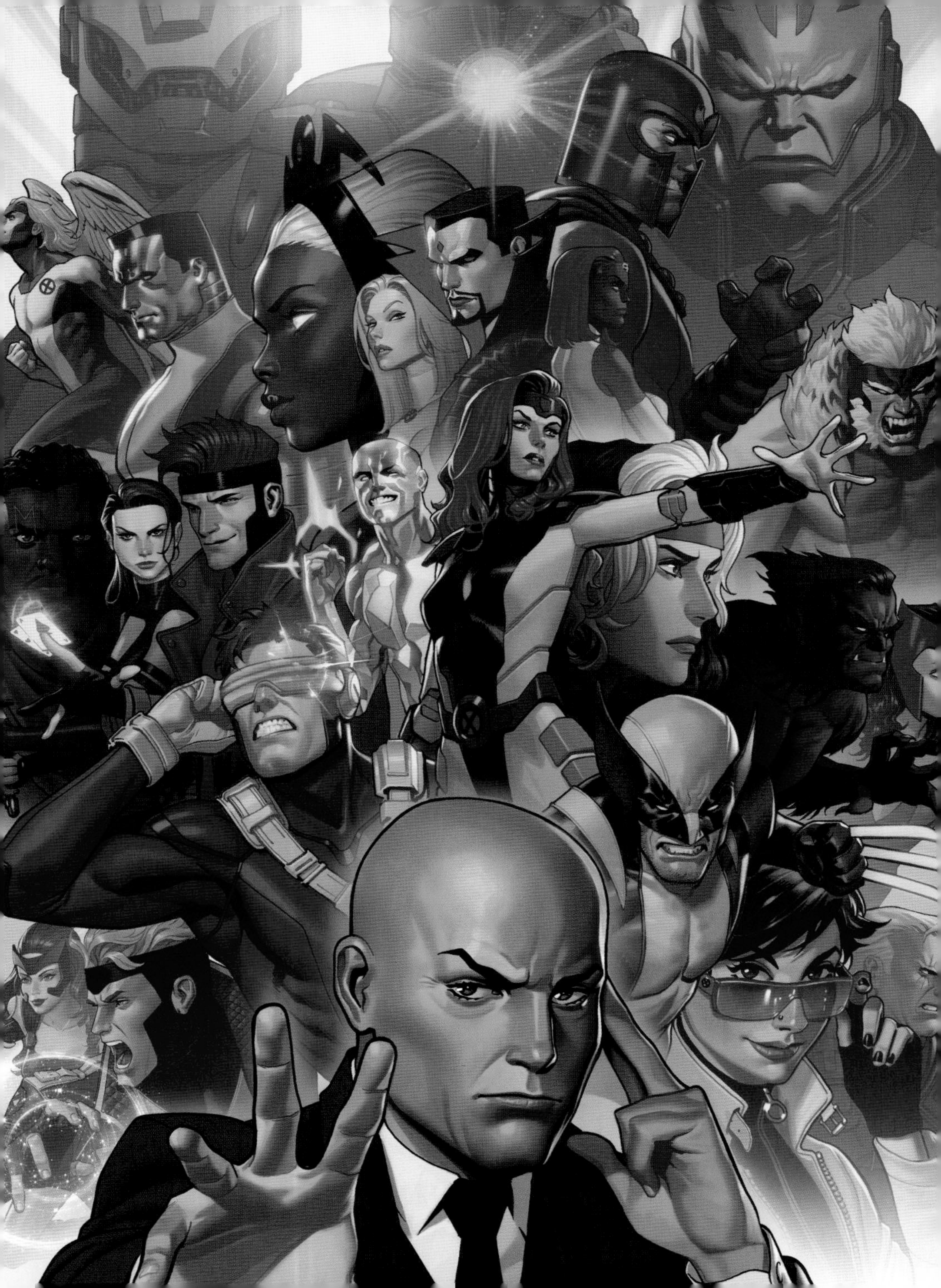

YOUR WEAKNESSES MAY ACTUALLY BE YOUR STRENGTHS

What you see as a fault may actually be the strongest part of you. This is one lesson that a team of mutants led by Professor Charles Xavier learned. Hated and feared, the mutants who became the X-Men were simply born with powers that were often misunderstood. Society deemed them unacceptable and unwelcome, yet it was their special abilities that often saved the people who shunned them.

The mutants themselves often feel uncomfortable in their own skin—seeing their differences as a weakness rather than empowering. Professor X tried to reverse this mindset by creating Xavier's School for Gifted Youngsters, to educate young mutants about their abilities and how to control them. Heroes like Rogue learned to use her destructive power to her advantage, while Cyclops emerged as a leader after learning to control his optic blasts.

We are often our own harshest critics. But what you see as a weakness in yourself, others may see as a gift. Uncomfortable being tall? A shorter person might yearn for your height. Worried about your slower skill set? Taking your time can be a blessing. Imagine being Professor X using Cerebro to find a mutant, and look keenly at your perceived shortcomings. You may realize how, in certain situations, they could be a great asset—and what make you exceptional.

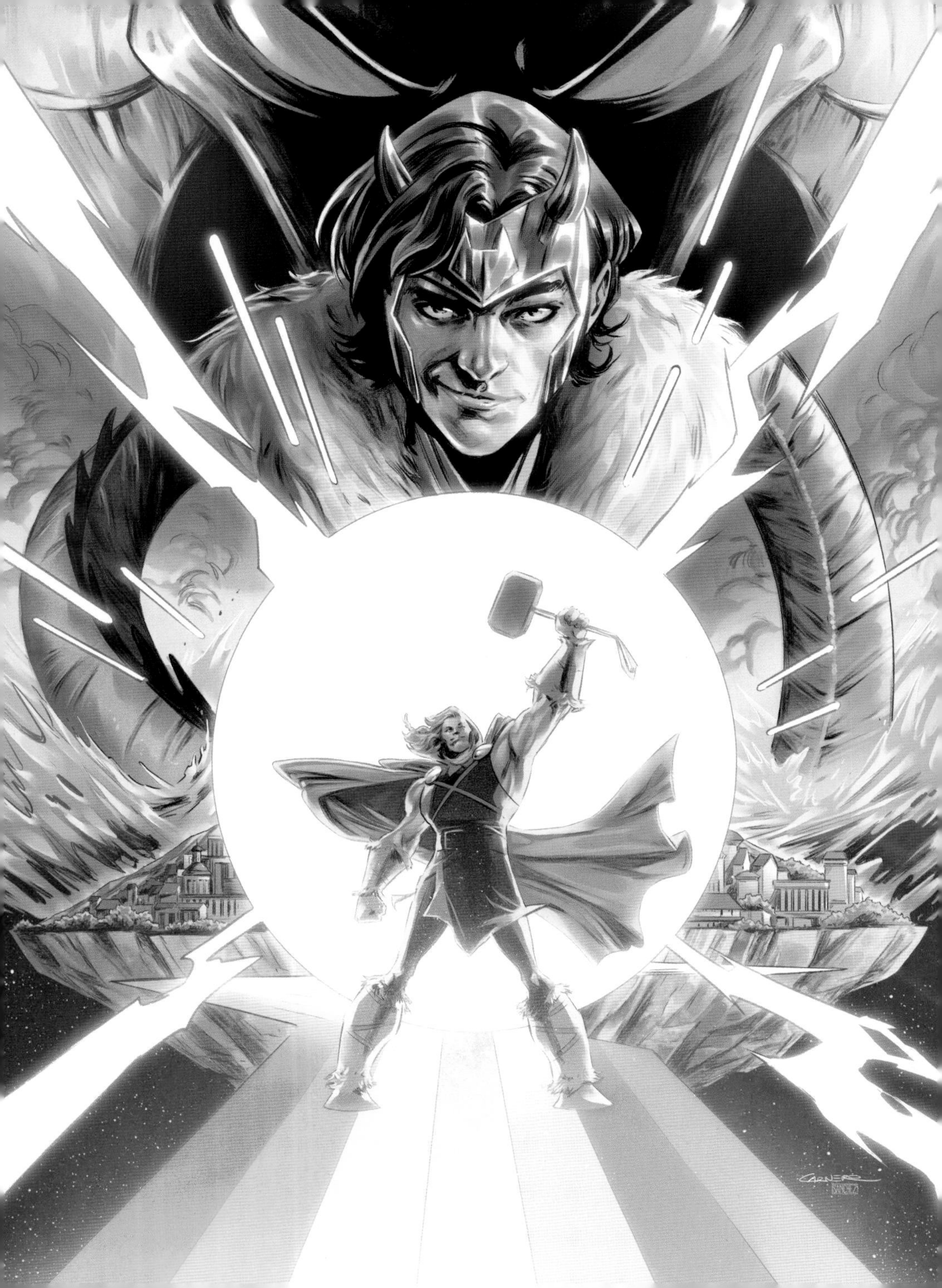

AGREE TO DISAGREE

There's nothing like a sibling squabble. Not getting along with a family member is a common problem to have—but when you're both deities from the realm of Asgard, things get a little more complicated. More often at odds than on the same page, brothers Thor and Loki have always had a love–hate relationship. In a classic brawn-versus-wit scenario, the two approach situations in their own ways: rarely agreeing, often miscommunicating, but always still having love for each other.

It's a sibling rivalry for the ages: The headstrong Thor rushes into a fight while Loki tends to play the fool's game, rigging the rules in his favor, just for sport. Loki's pranks often go too far, making bad situations even worse. Would you forgive someone for turning you into a frog to steal your royal throne? Probably not. But Thor did. (He was used to his brother's tricks; at least Thor in his frog form still had his hammer.) Thor and Loki rarely see eye to eye, but they always find a way to agree to disagree when it comes to achieving a shared goal.

You may not always agree with someone's ideals or actions, but try to find a middle ground (or Midgard, if you will). If that doesn't work, you can still find a way to work as a team despite having opposing points of view. Listen, learn, and lean into the other person's perspective. After all, if the two princes of Asgard can find a common ground, so can you.

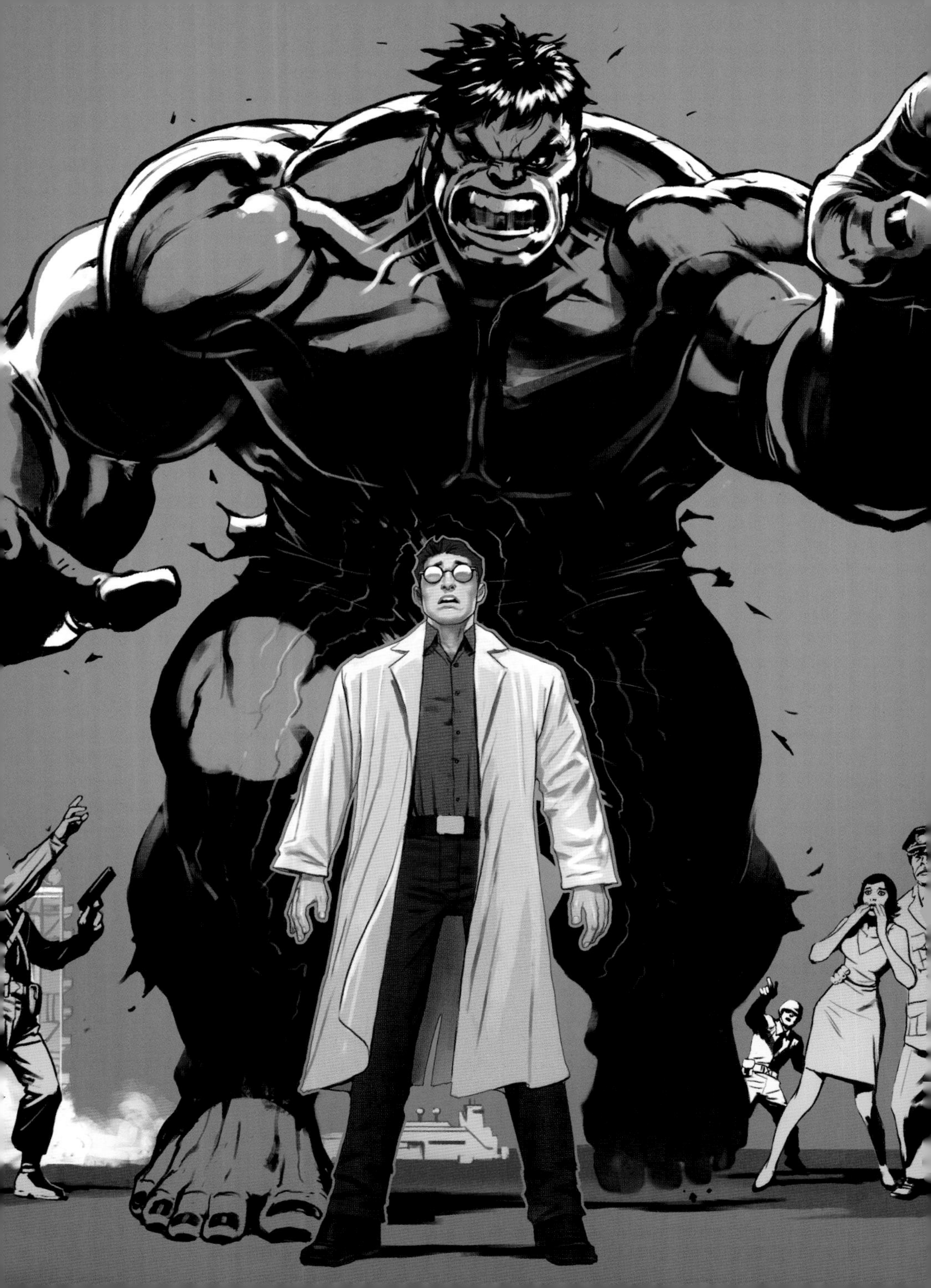

IT'S OKAY TO BE ANGRY SOMETIMES

HULK. SMASH. The monosyllabic green giant has a point. Don't bottle up your feelings; let them out. Let them out big. Having an outlet for your emotions allows you to make room for even deeper feelings, and that's a good thing. There's something cathartic about letting go completely, giving in to your rage, and just letting it all out.

The alter ego of scientist Bruce Banner materialized after he was exposed to high doses of gamma radiation. During Banner's moments of anger and stress, the Hulk emerges and lets loose in a way that mild-mannered Bruce could never. (I mean, if the Illuminati shot you into space, I'd think you'd be a little peeved too.) Yet the two sides complement each other. The Hulk's inability to hold back is what allows Bruce to be his mild-mannered self. And Hulk has learned how to channel and control his temper.

You might wish you had an alter ego who could do and say all the things you wish you could, but in the real world, there is only you—and you make the choice of how to react to stressful situations. There's no need to destroy city infrastructure or commit other random, chaotic destruction. It's healthy to express your feelings so they don't eat away at you, but balancing your inclination for outbursts with keeping your cool—while still conveying displeasure—is true emotional growth. I'd call that a smashing success.

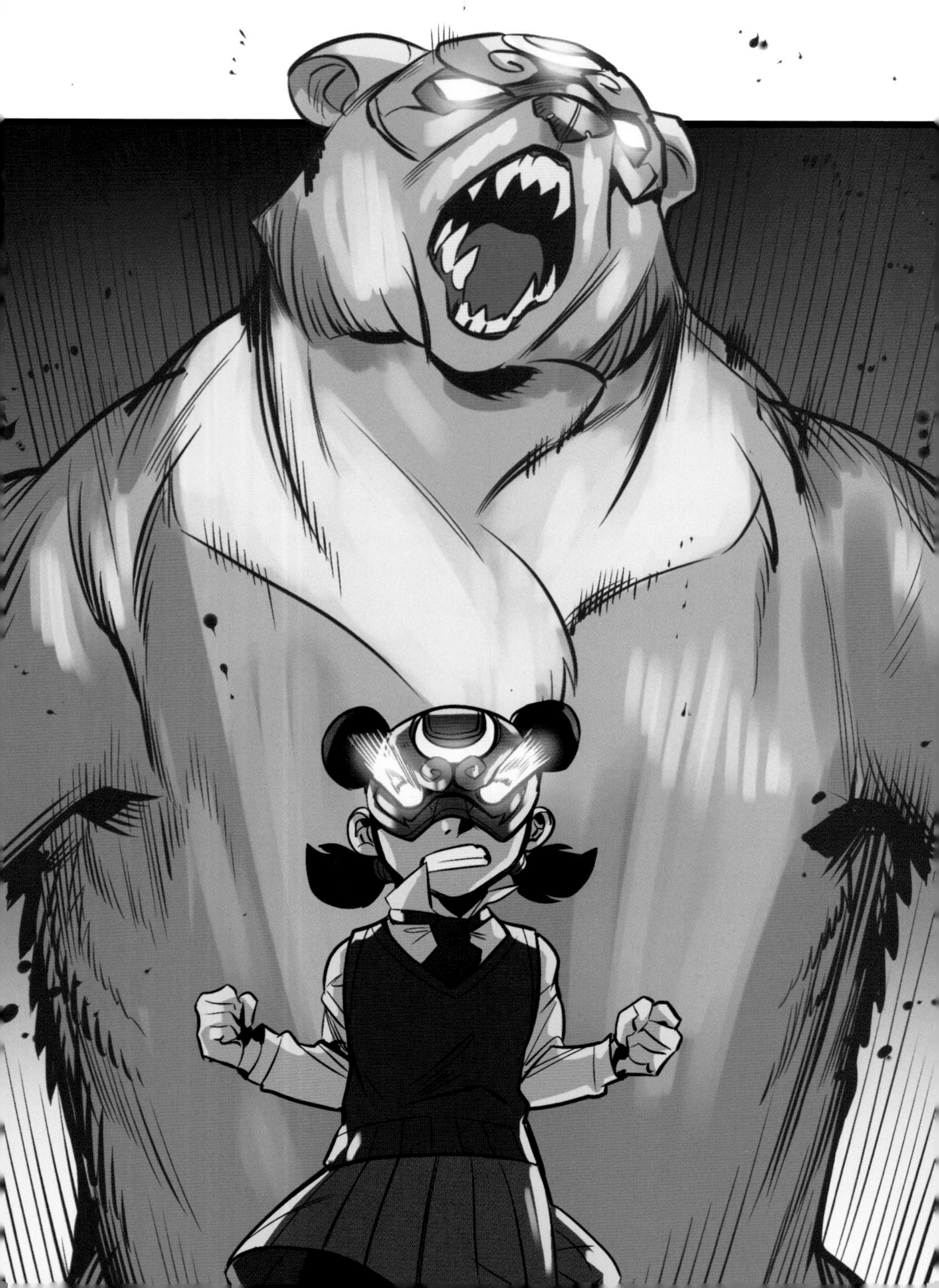

HARNESS THE POWER WITHIN

Seize the moment and find the strength within. Or in the case of Dan Bi, just summon your own magic bear. A tae kwon do prodigy, Dan Bi is able to invoke and control Io, a bear spirit who acts as her protector. The two shield each other from trouble and always have each other's backs. Being able to conjure a totem for strength helps Dan Bi navigate through life.

Taking on the name Crescent, Dan Bi calls forth Io through an enchanted mask, and their close bond makes the pair unstoppable. When Dan Bi gets bullied at school, she feels defeated. Summoning Io not only gives her extra bear-power to take on her antagonists but also gives her the confidence she needs to fight back.

Having an unshakeable sense of self takes practice; after all, no one is born with confidence (well, unless you're Tony Stark). So, when your anxiety rises at a crowded party, or your courage dips before a big presentation, summon your champion within. Finding inner strength can take just a moment of calm and a bear spirit to act as your avatar. But if you're not a child super hero named Crescent, encouragement from yourself, deep down, will work just fine.

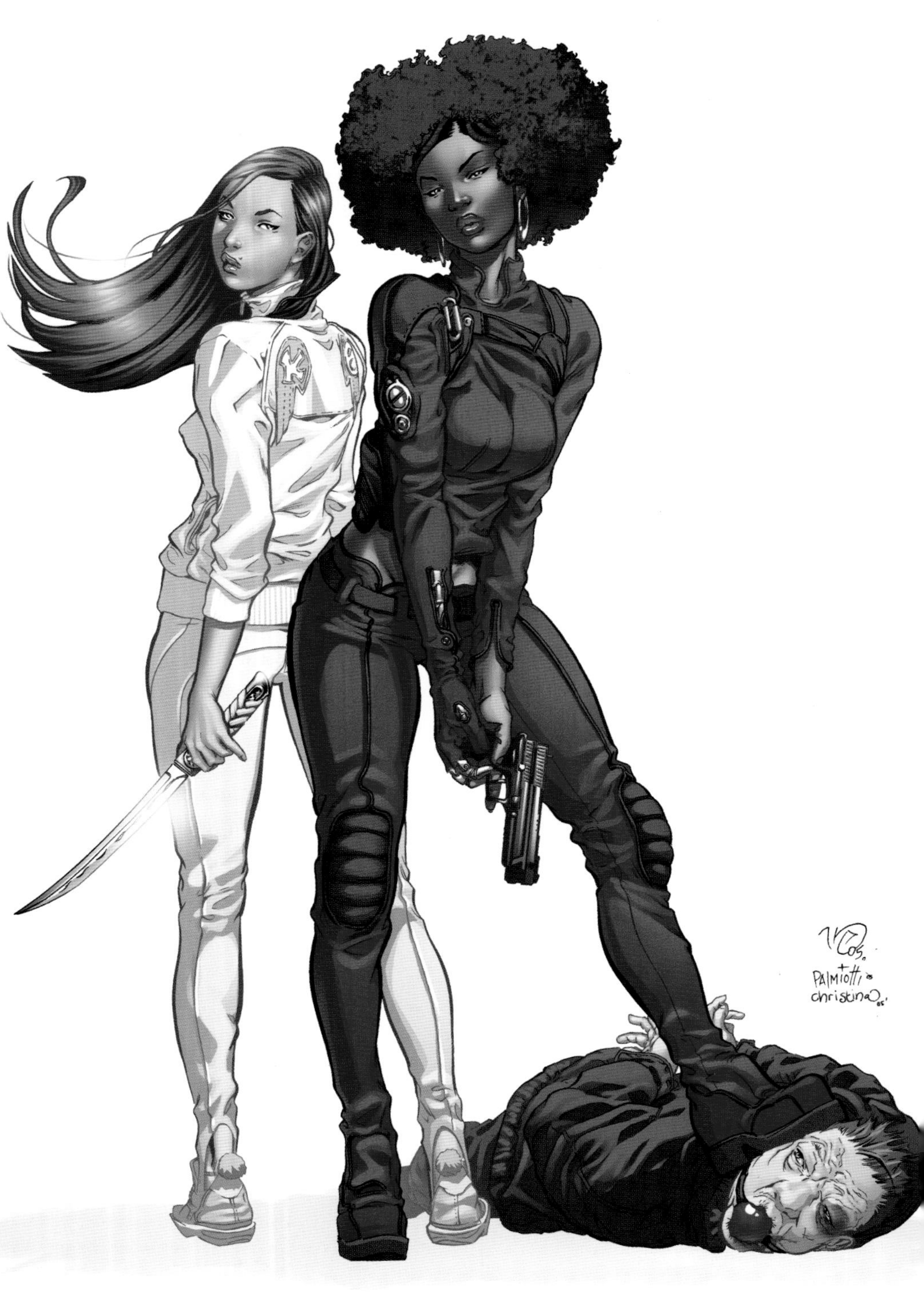
PALMIOTTI
christina

RESPOND WHEN NEEDED

Having someone you can depend on when things get tough can be just what you need. As Daughters of the Dragon, Misty Knight and Colleen Wing are the ultimate power duo. From forming their own private investigation firm, Knight-wing Restorations Ltd., to becoming bondswomen and bounty hunters, they've collaborated with everyone from Spider-Man to the X-Men. And working side by side, they always have each other's backs.

Misty's bionic arm gives her superhuman strength, making her a force on her own. But when she is paired with trained samurai Colleen, they become a powerful tag team. (Taking down an evil super villain who wears an 8-ball on his head? Misty and Colleen have you covered.) Like most formidable duos, they don't always see eye to eye, but these two best friends will run to each other's rescue, no questions asked.

No one has to go it alone. When someone calls upon you for help, be available for them. It takes a lot of strength to reach out, but even more to be the pillar someone else needs to lean on. Being there for a friend, in person or not, can make all the difference. Now, if you're asked to help take down the evil K'un L'un Steel Serpent, that's one thing, but agreeing to take someone to the airport, let's not get crazy—no one has the time for that chaos.

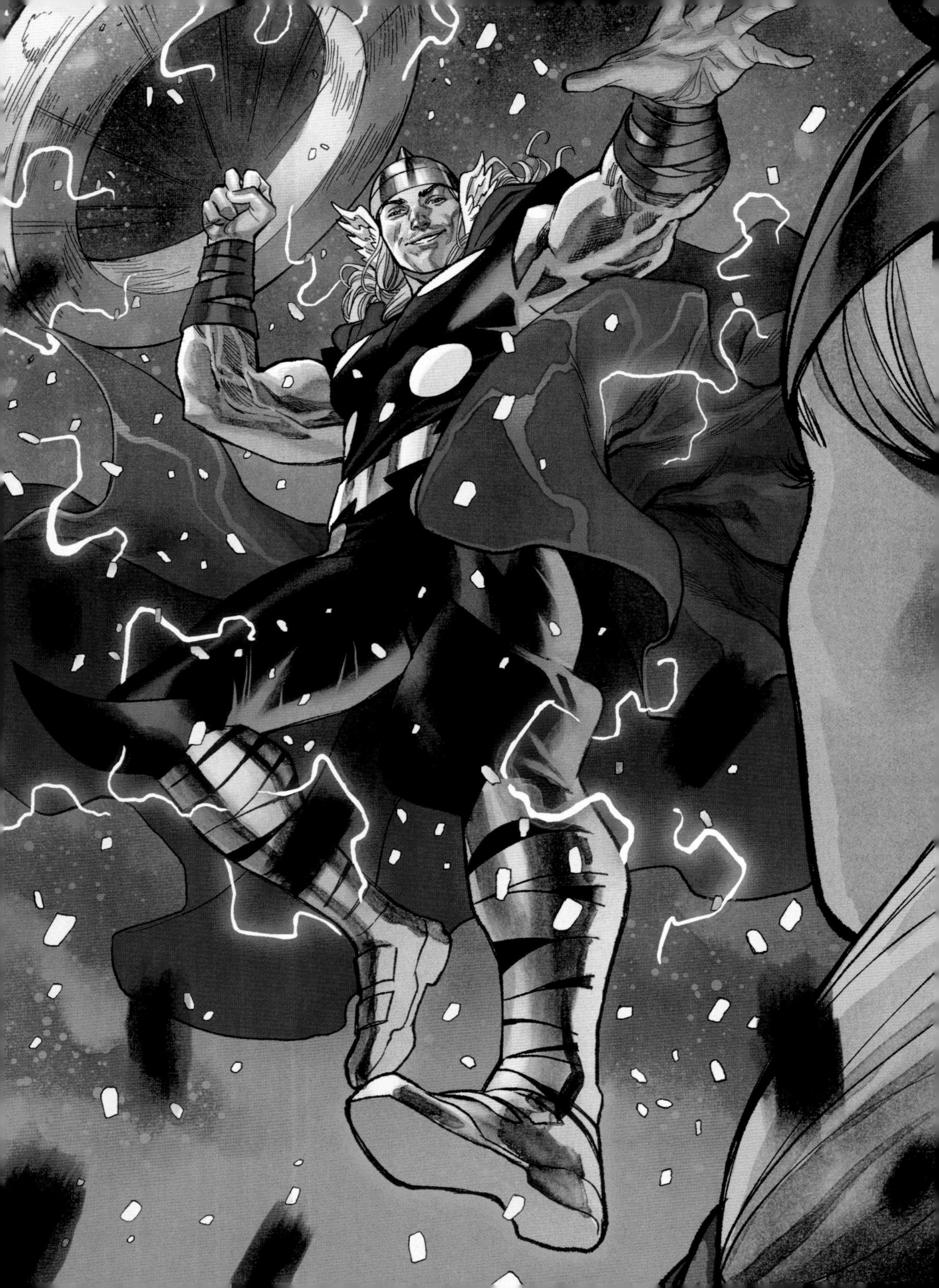

YOU ARE WORTHY

Even the God of Thunder can get the blues. As the Prince of Asgard, Thor has everything. Heir to the throne, a loyal crew of followers, and even the enchanted hammer, Mjolnir, that states under no uncertain terms that he is, in fact, worthy. Still, the Midgardian characteristic of doubt creeps its way into even the mind of the mighty one.

Thor's crisis of confidence happens after years of fighting, leaving him feeling lost and despondent. His emotional spiral is so deep that Thor loses his ability to carry Mjolnir, and even the thunder ignores him when he calls to it. The broken pieces of his former life become too much for him, to the point where he relinquishes his name and simply goes by Odinson. Then, just as Thor realizes that mortality is something that even he can't fight off for his Earthly companions, he understands that Mjolnir is just a metaphor of his self-worth.

Self-doubt can strike at any time. Sudden feelings of anxiety can appear out of nowhere. Understanding why you are feeling that way and figuring out how to overcome these fears are the first steps to defeating your own uncertainties. You don't need to lose the ability to wield a metaphorical hammer to know that being yourself is a work in progress—and that being open about your vulnerabilities is the strongest thing you can do.

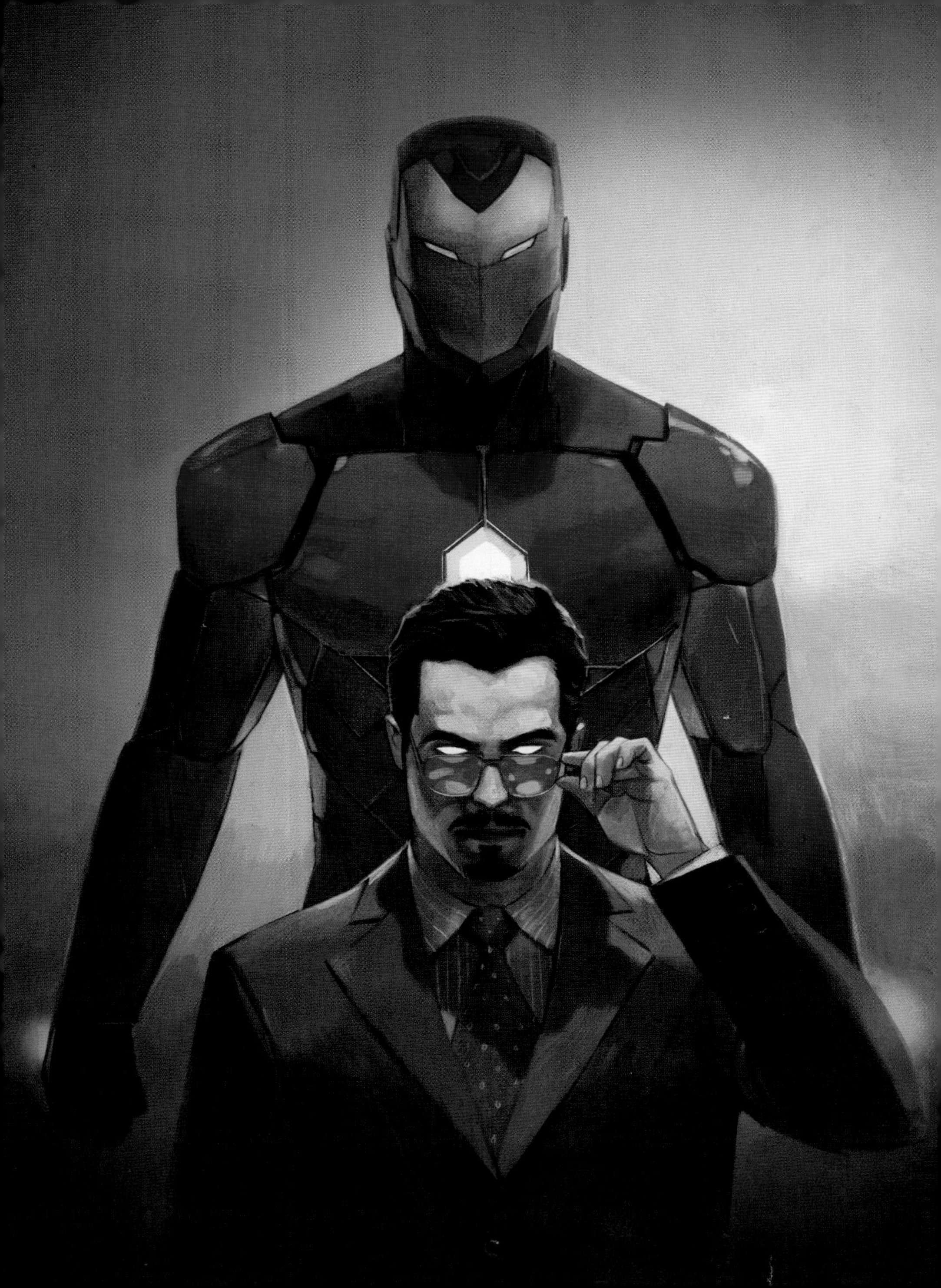

INVEST IN THE FUTURE

Remove the armor of the past and look toward the future. Even if you don't have access to the money or tech that a Stark nepo-baby has, it's important to figure out how to assemble opportunities to create a brighter tomorrow. Tony Stark is one of the world's most genius inventors, but it's his ability to solve problems before they even occur that places him high above the rest. As someone who is always looking ahead, he can almost predict the future.

Some futurists come across as crackpots or scaremongers, but Tony's heart and his arc reactor are in the right place. His choices may be controversial, but he just wants to create a better future for generations to come. This drives his innovation. With technology on his side, he is willing to take risks that others won't to ensure the safety of humanity.

No matter your status in society, making strides toward progress—financial, emotional, or physical—is essential. Looking ahead can be tough when you're in the weeds, but be like Tony and think ten steps ahead. In the long run, the dividends you can reap make the future worth investing in.

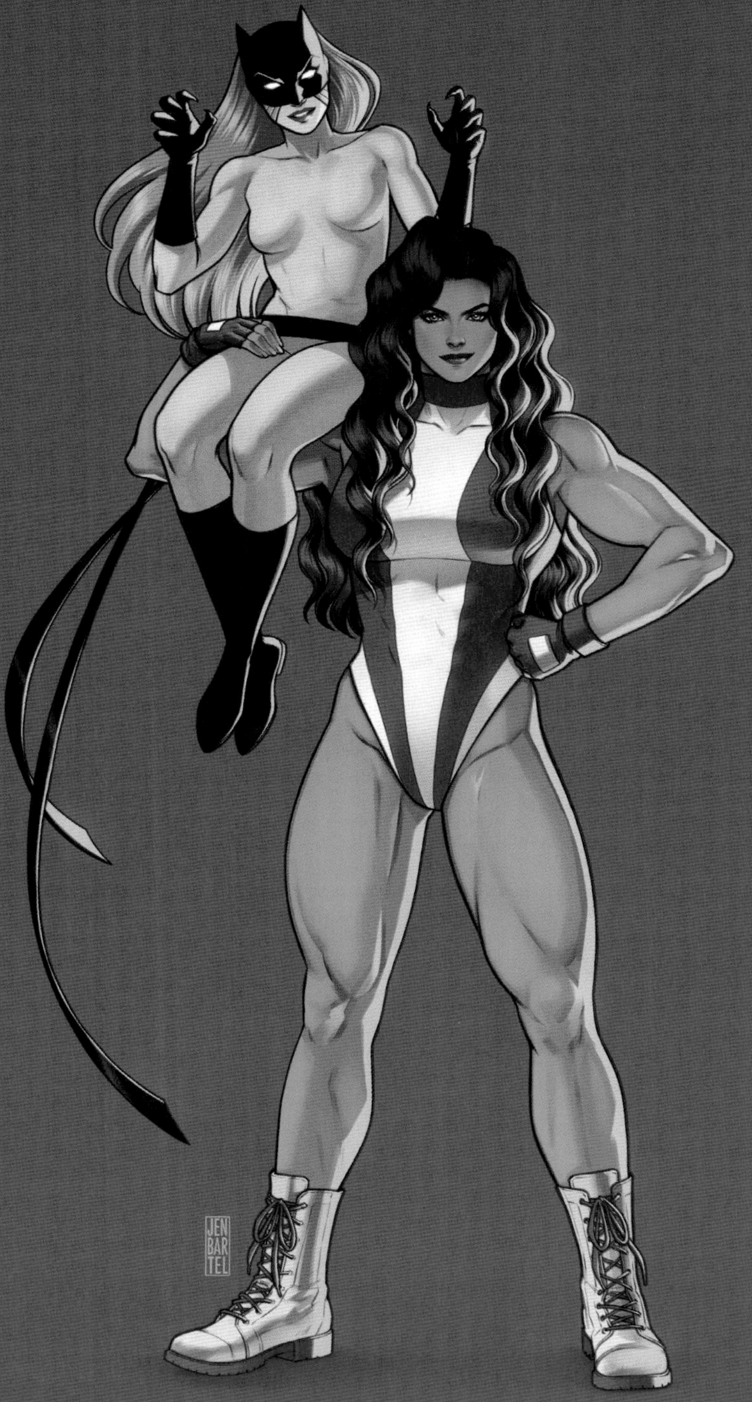
JEN
BAR
TEL

BE THERE FOR YOUR FRIENDS

Few things in life are better than sharing hot goss and eating cake with your best friend. Having a close pal to share your secrets, hear your woes, and just straight-up listen when you would rather Hulk out can be a real lifesaver. Jennifer Walters and Patsy Walker met at work and, like most professional pals, they bonded instantly over office politics and the aforementioned gossip. (Even in the Marvel world, you can't escape work drama.)

As the super heroes She-Hulk and Hellcat, Jen and Patsy deal with both workplace headaches and hero hurdles. Whether it's Jen advising against Patsy's wanting to destroy an A.I.M. base or Patsy rushing to Jen's side when she falls into a post-battle coma, these two are friendship goals. They fight hard, karaoke even harder, and will always be each other's biggest supporter.

A trusted friend relationship isn't just where you can share your insecurities—the best part is being there for the other person as they go through their own troubles. Whether it's talking about your terrible boss, or discussing how your mortal enemy is the worst super villain ever, showing up as an active and supportive part of a friend's life is its own reward. And when it's your turn to vent, sitting down with a true friend is the best form of therapy—and if there's cake involved, consider most of your problems already solved.

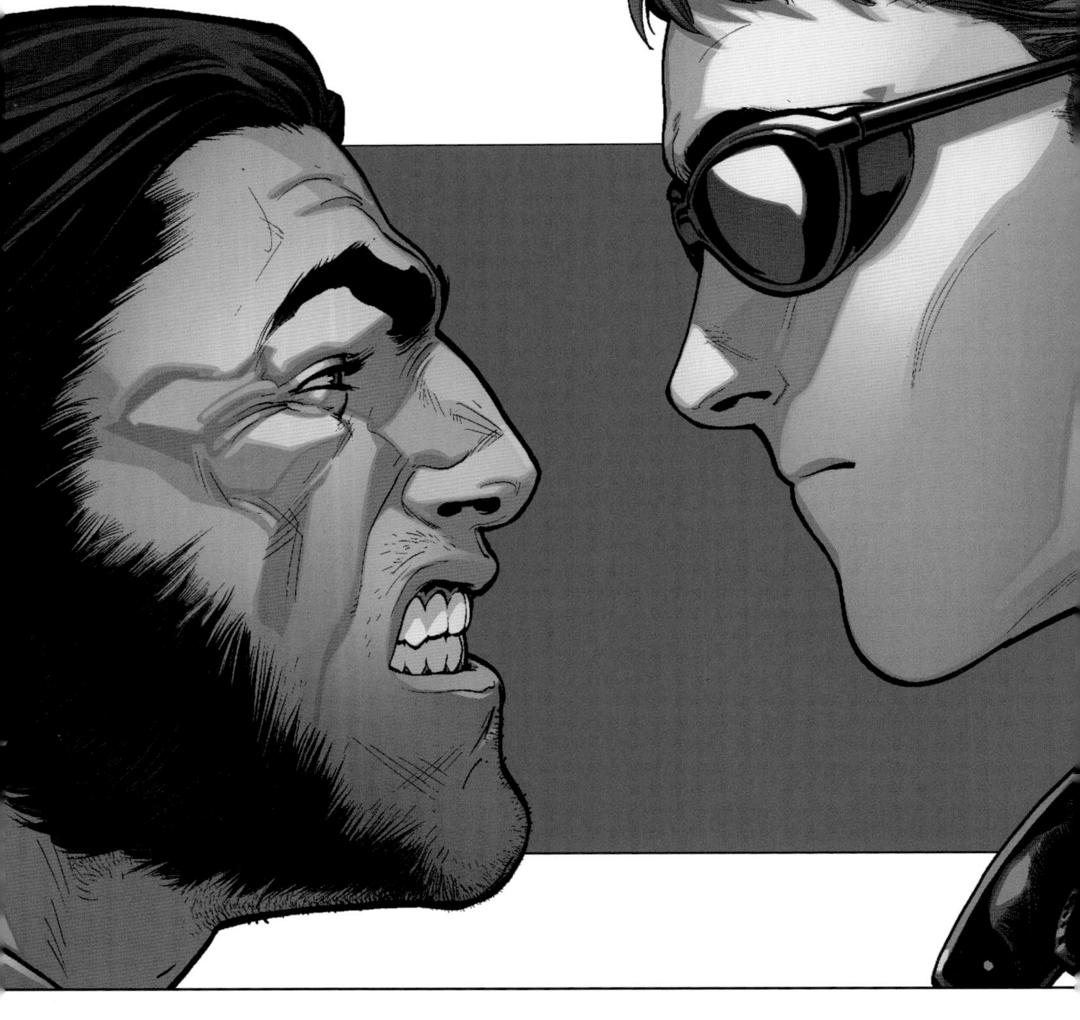

LEARN TO WORK
WITH OTHERS

Being nice at work is all fun and games until the adamantium claws come out. You might get paired up with an outgoing person, while you're more of an introvert. Or your partner could be messy and disorganized, while you prefer a perfectly filed, color-coded lifestyle. Or maybe . . . you get paired up with someone who has a big ego and morals that are the complete opposite of yours, and just happens to be dating the girl of your dreams. Speaking hypothetically, of course. Or not, if we're talking about Wolverine and Cyclops.

Forever at odds, these frenemies always find a way to put aside their differences to get the job done, then immediately pick their grudges right back up. When Cyclops lets Idie Okonkwo—a young mutant whom Wolverine has taken under his wing—take out members of the Hellfire Club, Wolverine realizes he and Cyclops have two different visions for the future of mutants: While Logan's goal has been to protect the mutant children, Cyclops will do anything and use anyone to win fights. This causes Wolverine to leave the X-Men and form the Jean Grey School for Higher Learning. But ultimately, even this rift between teammates is bridged once again for the common good . . . until the next time they disagree.

Having a difference of opinion can be difficult in friendship, with family, or even at work. Resolution takes time, patience, and sometimes keeping your own ego in check. So turn down those optic blasts, because you may learn something from the opposing view that will change your opinion. Compromise can lead to solving problems, both in the mutant world and our own.

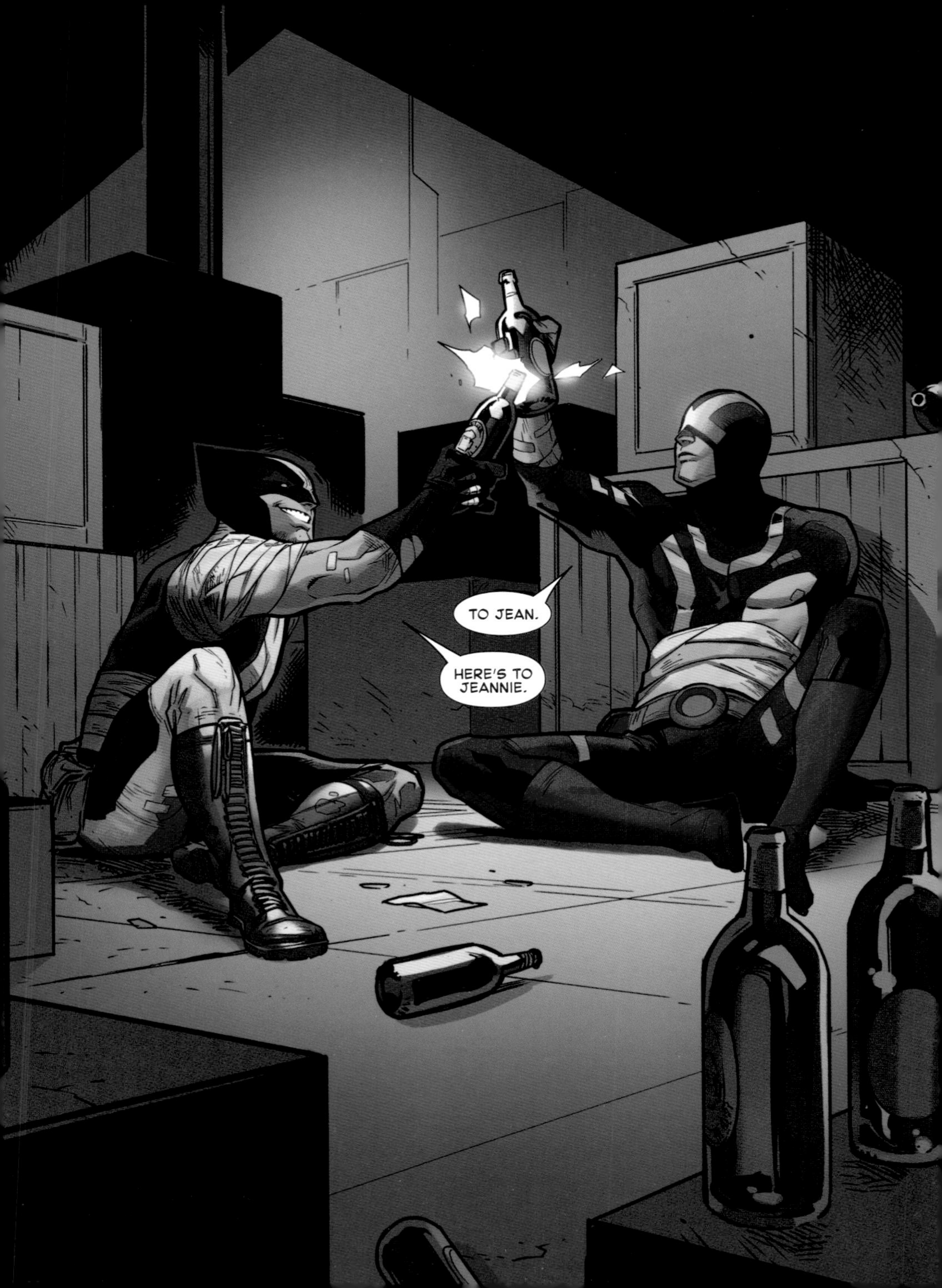
TO JEAN.
HERE'S TO JEANNIE.

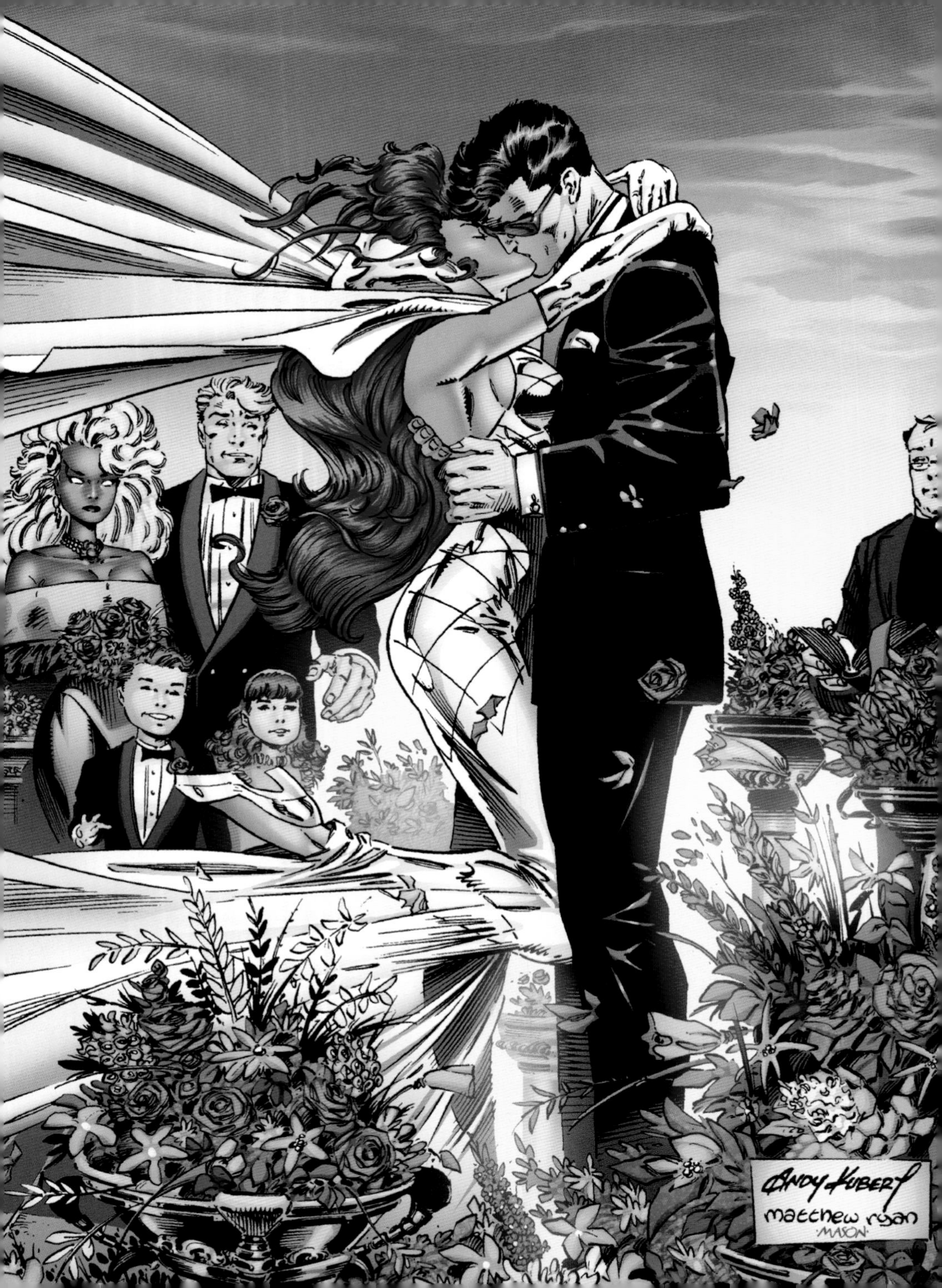
ANDY KUBERT
matthew ryan
·MASON·

NEVER WASTE AN OPPORTUNITY TO TELL SOMEONE YOU LOVE THEM

Before it's too late, before your loved one leaves to buy groceries and gets encompassed by the Phoenix Force, tell them you love them. The Jean Grey–Scott Summers love story is legendary. They started out together as students at Xavier's School for Gifted Youngsters under the tutelage of Professor X, who taught them and other mutants to harness their powers. With a strong telepathic bond beyond just a mental connection, Jean and Scott had a love relationship that included the highest of highs and the lowest of lows, culminating in their wedding at the X-Mansion, where they first connected.

The couple has had a whiplash romance for the ages, but through it all, their love was a constant—until Jean merged with the Phoenix Force, upending their storybook tale. At one point, when Jean is presumed dead, Scott shuts off his emotions, not allowing himself to feel at all so as not to succumb to grief—only to be surprised that she is actually alive. Even as the Dark Phoenix takes over and their relationship is put to the ultimate test, Jean is always the endgame for Scott.

Whether fleeting or everlasting, love is one of our most complicated and wonderful human emotions, even if you're not a hero with mutant powers. So when you're right in the middle of love, give into it. Tell the person how you feel—don't wait for the perfect moment. Scott loved Jean so much he ended up marrying her clone—don't do that. Instead, express your adorations to someone who reciprocates your exact feelings so that you don't live with regret. Love is a powerful force, indeed.

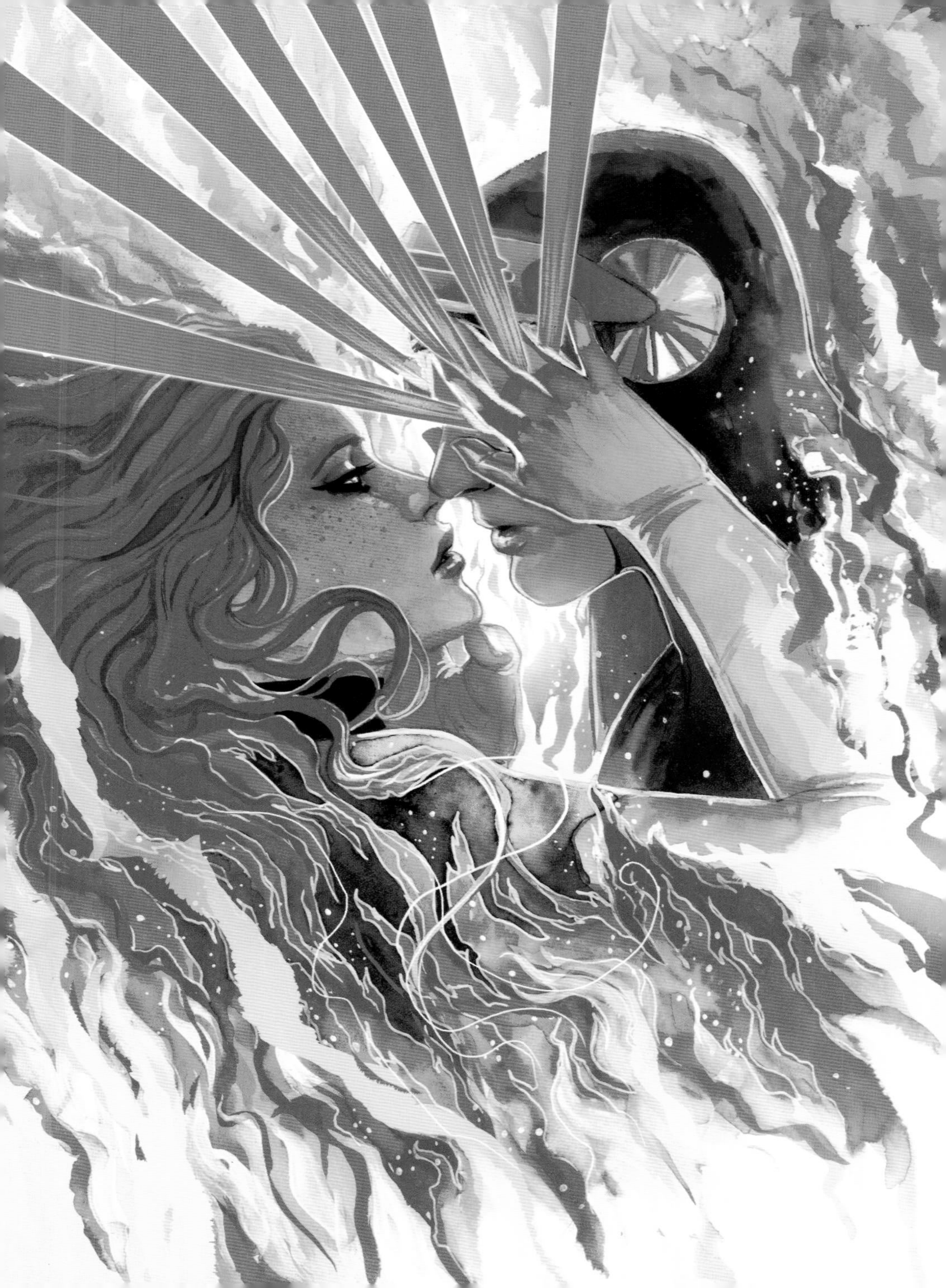

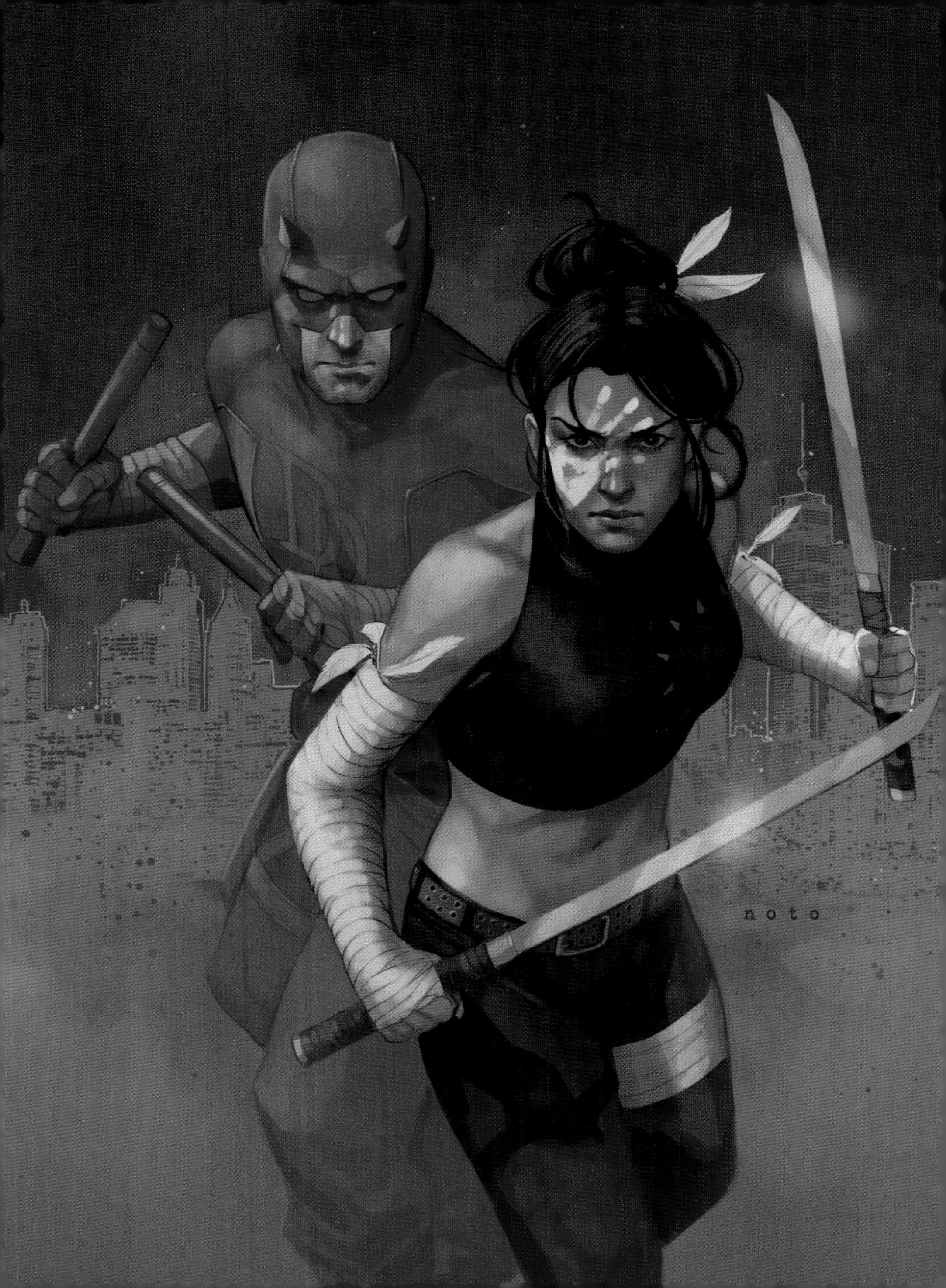
noto

MAKE PEACE WITH YOUR PAST

Moving on is never easy. Take, for example, Maya Lopez, "Echo"—a deaf woman who, as a child, lost her beloved father at the hand of his employer, Wilson Fisk, A.K.A. Kingpin. Fisk becomes Maya's guardian and sees potential in her, training her and advancing her fighting skills. Dedicating her life to her new father figure, Maya soon realizes that he may not be as he seems.

When Maya finds out that it is actually Kingpin who is responsible for her father's death, she starts to doubt the motives for her ruthless past. Maya must reconcile with the villainous acts she performed in the name of loyalty. Acknowledging her actions, she finds the grace to forgive herself, turns over a new leaf, and begins fighting crime.

Guilt is hard to shake. There will be times when you think you won't be able to forgive yourself—but it's the only way to move on. Maya passes judgment on her past and then makes peace with herself. Give yourself the space to forgive yourself, which will help clear your way forward. It will only make you stronger.

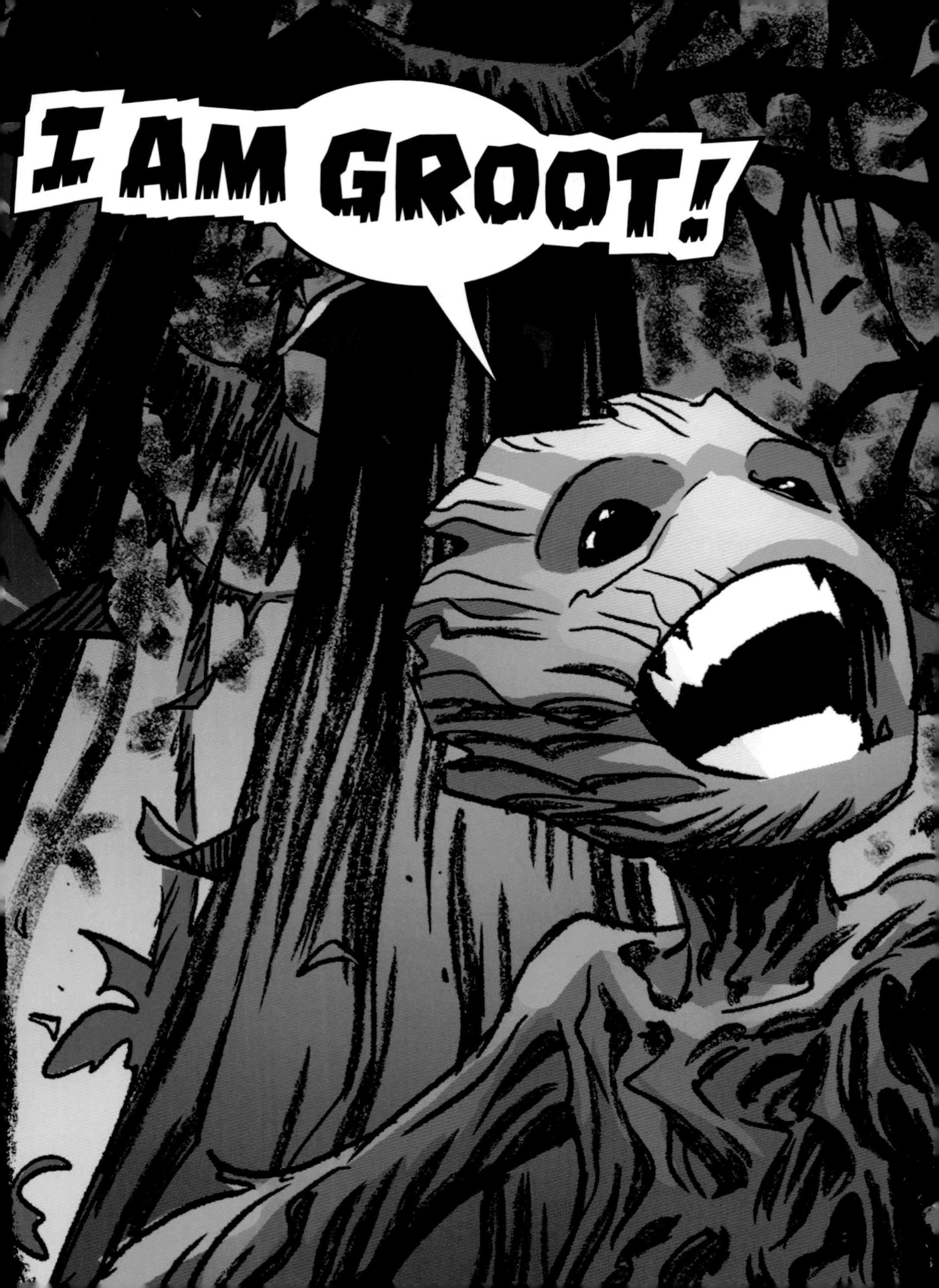
I AM GROOT!

THERE'S ALWAYS ROOM FOR GROWTH

Monster? Tree? Monster Tree? Nope, he . . . is . . . Groot. A creature from Planet X and a core member of the Guardians of the Galaxy, Groot can extend his limbs to defend and protect. If Groot gets destroyed, he can regenerate after being replanted, recovering all of his memories. Groot's resurrection abilities are a metaphor for rebuilding and moving forward.

At his biggest, Groot stands 23 feet tall and weighs more than 8,000 pounds. But size isn't everything. Post Annihilation War, amid a fight with Phalanx security drones, Groot sacrifices himself to save the team. But Groot lives on as a sapling, not quite as foreboding but still a menace and just as valuable to his team as his full-grown self. The important thing is, he lives to fight another day.

An identity rebirth doesn't have to be a 180-degree transformation; just realizing what you need to do to change your attitude or circumstances means you've already taken the steps needed to evolve. Once you've taken stock of the change you need, it's time to repair what might be broken, be it interpersonal relationships, ambitions, or mistakes that need mending. Note that applying these lessons is a work in progress. It's easy to get dismayed by setbacks or be too hard on yourself. Just remember: You. Are. Groot. Life is all about learning to grow and evolve.

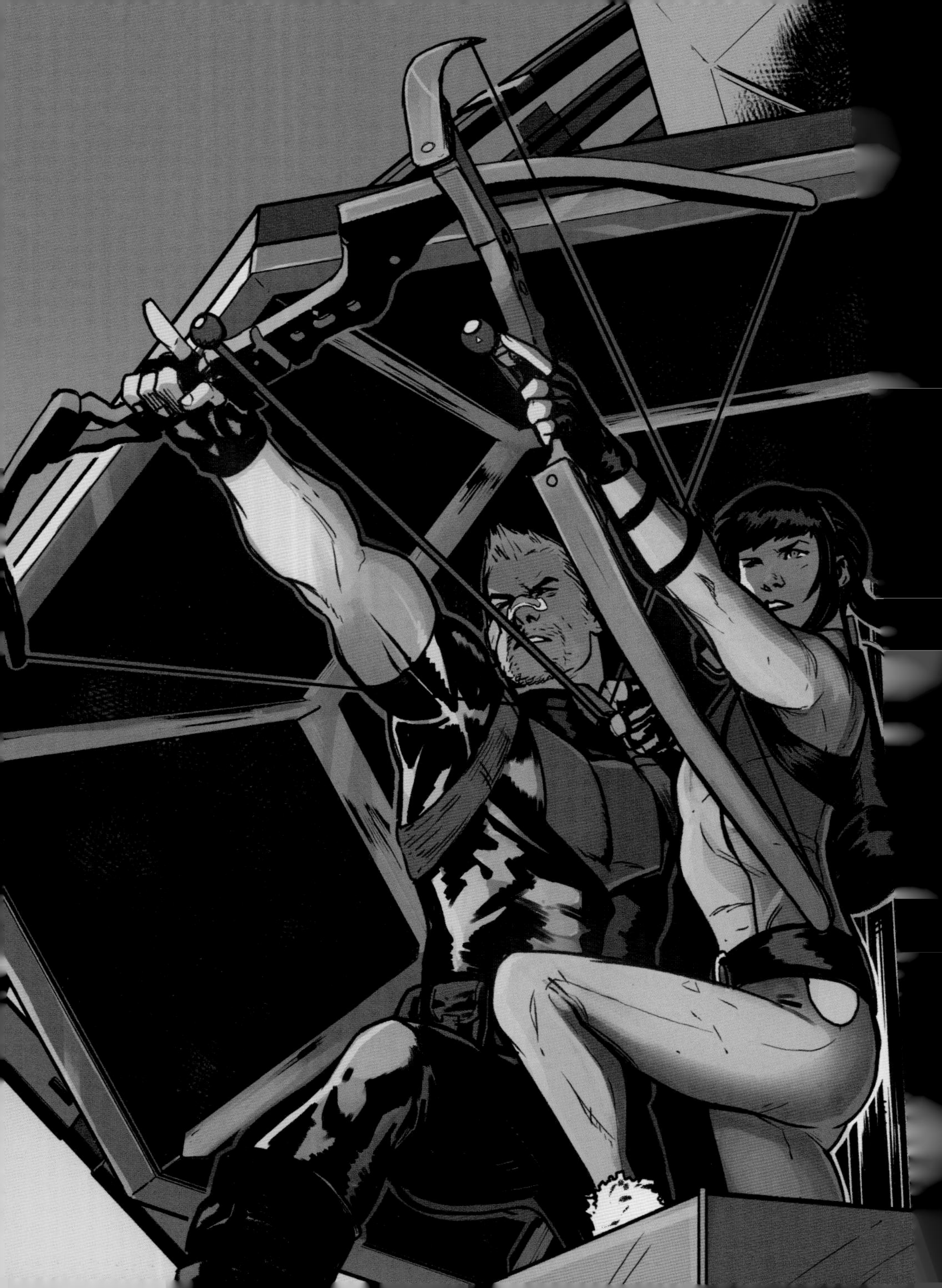

BE INSPIRED

Mentorship matters. When Kate Bishop's mother, Eleanor, dies, and the criminal activities of her father, Derek, are revealed, Kate's world crumbles. Yet she takes it upon herself to decline her family's wealth and follow a path of selfless heroism. She finds inspiration in Hawkeye and Jessica Jones, two people who lead the way in motivating Kate to become her own hero.

Kate looks up to Avenger Clint Barton, A.K.A. Hawkeye, whose absence of super powers resonates with her own. Admiring him for his focus and perseverance, she finds him to be a valuable mentor and then a friend. Jessica Jones proves to be another role model for Kate, allowing her to share her most traumatic secrets and showing her how to provide a safe emotional space. By observing and absorbing her mentors' best attributes, Kate takes their guidance to heart.

Finding someone who you can look up to is essential to your growth and success. Use your hero's power moves as inspiration to create your own journey. Kate found inspiration from two very different heroes who showed her how to navigate life in her own unique way. Engage with people you admire, understand how they navigate the ups and downs of their lives and careers, and apply these discoveries to your own life. Even if you don't follow the same path, their wisdom can help shape you into the hero you aspire to be.

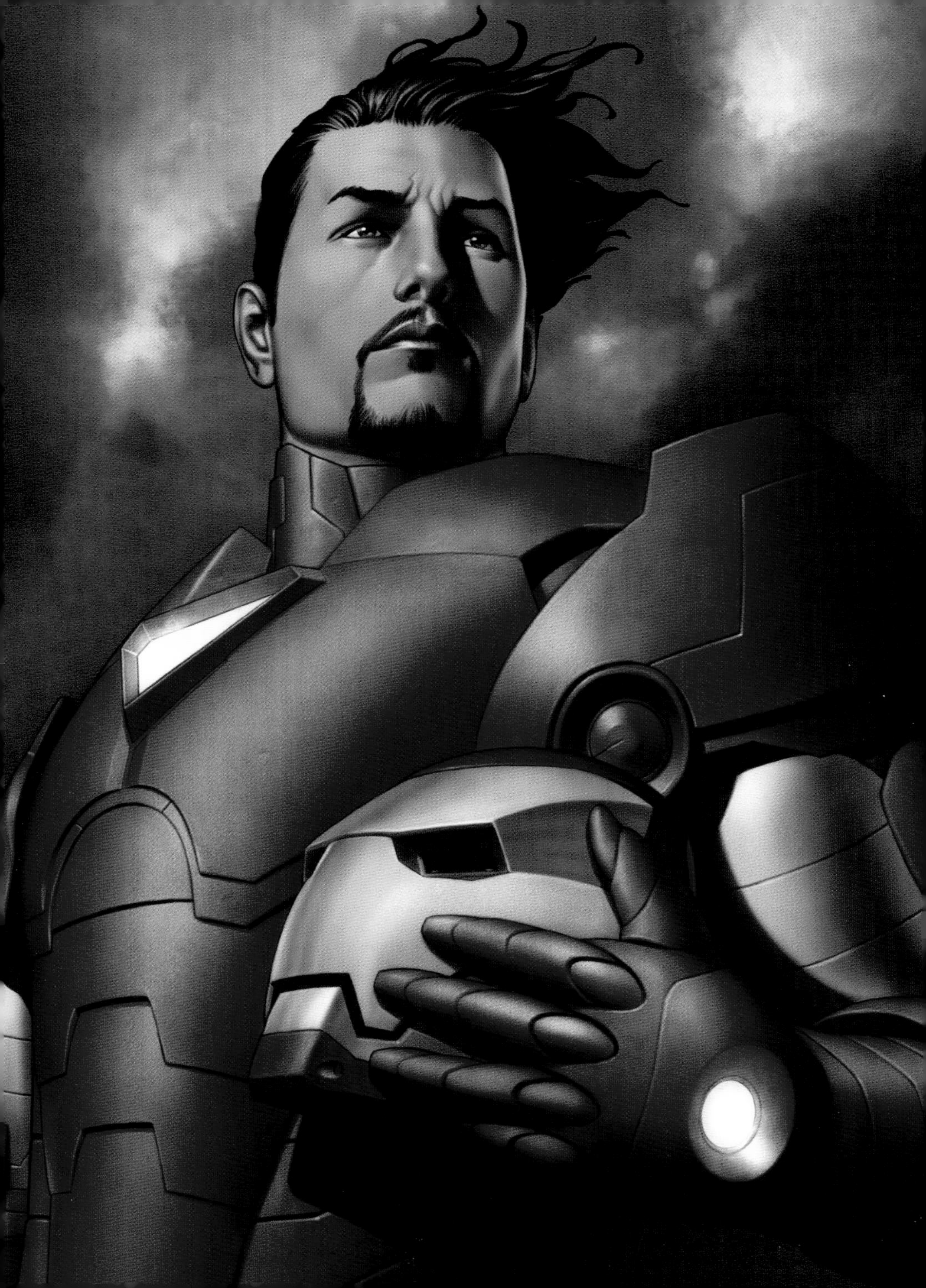

BE A HERO

Being a hero includes accepting failure and responsibility for one's mistakes. Tony Stark is known for being brash, self-centered, and always over the top. A figure almost too loud to be an inspiration, nevertheless he is one because when push comes to shove, he'll try to do what is right and decent. This becomes clear to him when a Celestial must decide whether Earth is worth saving. Tony ventures forth to meet its true face, where he is forced to confront his wrongdoings.

Facing his worst failures head on, Tony realizes that his past has led to his present, and his mistakes are what has built his character. At the same time, the Celestial looks at the world through Tony's eyes and learns that what makes a human . . . well, a human is that there is room for redemption. Tony sees how his decisions—right or wrong—can change the future, and the best way to lead is by example, by striving to do what is right and accepting when he is wrong.

Doing what is honorable is never as black and white as it seems. But attempting to do your best for what is righteous is always commendable, even if you sometimes fail. Mistakes give you an opportunity to learn. Wins give you an opportunity to take things to the next level. As Iron Man, Tony Stark accepts intergalactic challenges. As Tony, even without the suit, he steps up to be a good example. Be an inspiration to others. Mentor, lead, and most importantly, learn. These are the qualities of a hero.

ACKNOWLEDGMENTS

Thank you to my own personal first family of Marvel, Alice Kawakami; Kyle, Tyler, and Mason Fujikawa; and Mark Kawakami. To the team I would assemble to fight on Earth-616 and beyond, Mel Caylo, Cheryl deCarvalho, Chrissy Dinh, Chrys Hasegawa, Sarah Kuhn, and Robb Pearlman. To the heroes with whom I would fight villainy, then eat cake, Kristin Baver, AJ Camarillo, and Kim Trinh. To the powerful pair who guided me along this journey, thank you, Elizabeth Smith and Leah Wilson. To the Squadron Supreme at Marvel, Sven Larsen, Sarah Singer, Jeremy West, and Jeff Youngquist. Finally, to my kids: Remember to think before you Hulk-smash.

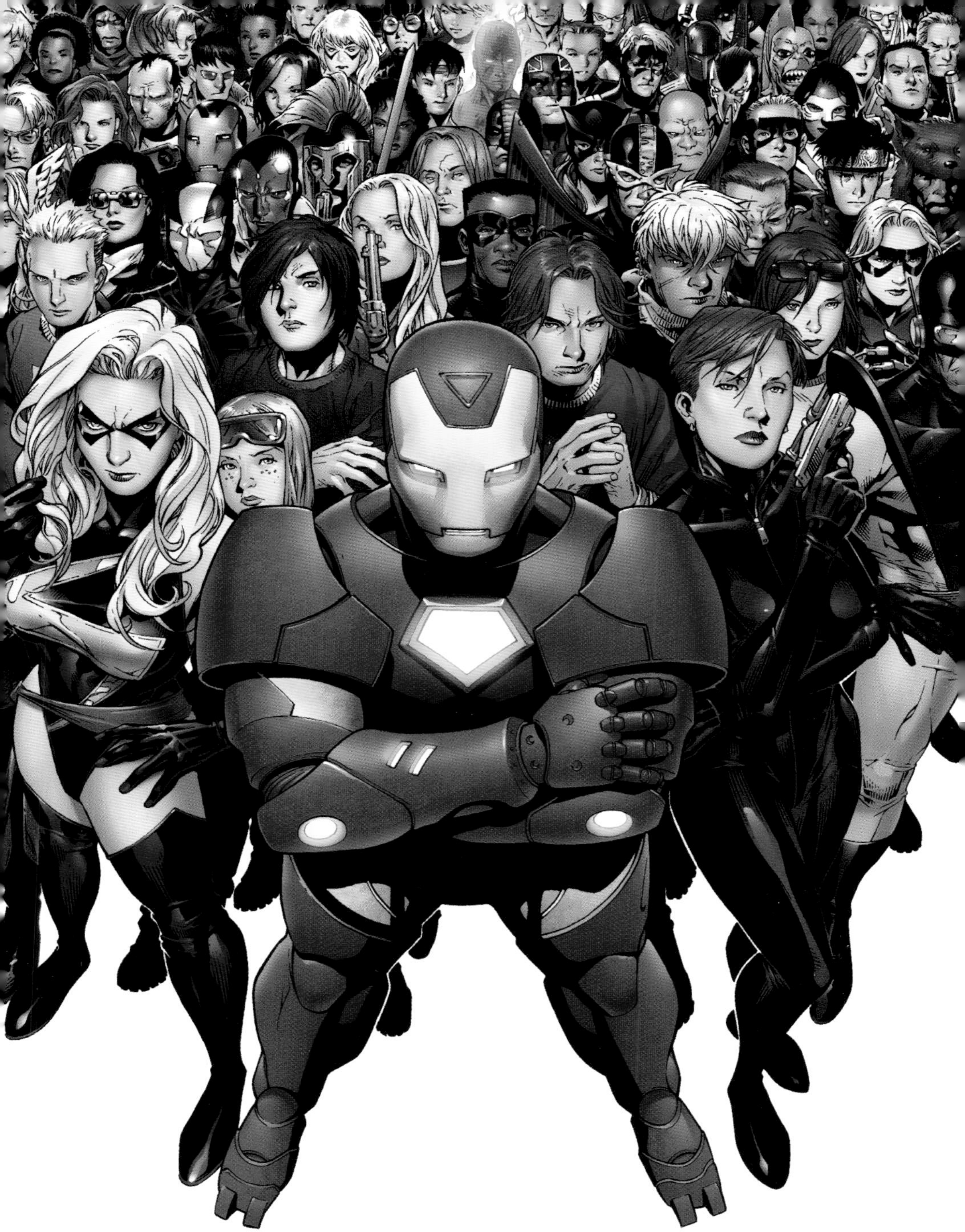

ABOUT THE AUTHOR

Jenn Fujikawa is a lifestyle and pop culture author, content creator, and host. She has worked with Lucasfilm, Marvel, Disney, and more. Jenn is the author of multiple fandom-based books including *Star Wars: The Life Day Cookbook*, *Ghostbusters: The Official Cookbook*, *Parks and Recreation: The Official Cookbook*, and *The Princess Bride: The Official Cookbook*, and is the co-author of Marvel's *Great Responsibility: Raising Your Little Hero from Toddler to Teen* with Troy Benjamin, and many more. For more of her adventures, check out her Instagram @justjennrecipes.